Opening Night
Jacque Brel....
24 January 1989

Dear Joan
Many, many Thanks
for the beautiful
costumes.
The show is stunning

Hugh Murphy

CLOTHES LINES

Julia McKenzie
CLOTHES LINES

OFF-THE-PEG STORIES
FROM THE CLOSETS
OF THE FAMOUS

**All Royalties to The Alan Page
Heart Foundation**

 Robson Books

First published in Great Britain in 1988 by Robson Books Ltd,
Bolsover House, 5–6 Clipstone Street, London W1P 7EB

Copyright © 1988 Julia Mckenzie

British Library Cataloguing in Publication Data

Clothes line: off the peg anecdotes.
    1. Celebrities' clothing
    I. Mckenzie, Julia
    646.3

ISBN 0 86051 557 5

The anecdotes in this book were kindly donated by our contributors to THE
ALAN PAGE HEART FUND, to whose fund-raising efforts all royalties will
be given.

Printed in Great Britain by St Edmundsbury Press Ltd, Bury St Edmunds,
Suffolk.
Bound by Dorstel Press Ltd, Harlow, Essex

FOREWORD

The acting profession is notoriously fraught with hazards, from unemployment to bad notices, from over-exposure to under-exposure. But one of the worst is the constant bombardment of begging letters actors receive; requests for photographs, autographs, things to auction, personal appearances, and last but not least, requests for a recipe, recollection, or (hardest of all) the amusing anecdote for the slim volume ... all for charity of course. Now I've joined the band of supplicants, and I can only express my deep gratitude to all the dear and kind people who responded to my letters. I also sincerely hope they won't *all* write and ask the same of me.

All the royalties from this book will go to the Alan Page Heart Fund, a charity founded by the Follies Company. To give you an idea how it all started I can do no better than to quote from a piece that Diana Rigg wrote for the programme of one of the fund-raising events, an evening of Stephen Sondheim's music which was the culmination of a year's work for this charity.

'Alan was a dear man. Modest and professional, like so many that constitute the backbone of English musical theatre. For years he was in the chorus of Covent Garden, and earlier worked with Julia McKenzie in *Mame*, and long before that, was in *Camelot* when Cameron Mackintosh worked as an assistant stage manager on it. He came to an open audition of *Follies* and Cameron, recognising him, immediately said 'I want that man for Roscoe.' Alan was so stunned he had to sit down to recover from the shock.

His wife had recently died, and the bustle of *Follies* rehearsals was a welcome distraction from his loss. Habitually pushing his spectacles back in place, he got on with the job. We were due to preview in a week, the set was troublesome, script changes were being made ... the usual pre-opening scramble. Nevertheless, time was found to hold a Fourth of July party for the Americans in the company. Alan was there quietly enjoying himself. It was the last time we were to see him. He died of a heart attack the next day.

The company was stunned, but tradition is unwavering. A replacement was found and the show opened. Circumstances had denied us the means of expressing our affection for Alan and sadness at his death. So as soon as possible it was decided to start the Alan Page Heart Fund, the proceeds to go towards buying equipment for his local hospital. The first fund-raising event was a jumble sale. For weeks beforehand the actors tottered to the theatre with a variety of carrier bags, bundles and cases. A vast amount of clothes and bric-a-brac resulted and battle commenced in the Grand Circle bar between shows one Saturday. An amazing £486 was raised in fifty minutes. The bargains and the buys were spectacular. Jo Gordon bought a saucy pair of patchwork trousers and Evan Pappas purchased a bright ginger tweed three-piece suit that only a man of unshakeable confidence could carry off. It was all great fun.

Next on the agenda was a carol concert held outside the theatre one evening. The band gallantly played in the chill night air while the company sang and Lisa, Dawn, Vanessa and the other dancers (acknowledged the prettiest line-up in London) cajoled passers-by and pounded on drivers trapped at the lights. It was all in wonderful spirit and what's more we collected £242.

Julia, Simon and Gillian had the idea to present an evening's entertainment of Stephen Sondheim's music.'

That evening raised twenty thousand pounds, and the Fund was now well on its way. Then I had the idea for this book chatting backstage between scenes one day. The recollection of an outfit or stage costume seemed to strike an immediate chord, and the stories came tumbling out. So it was into action with the begging letters.

In due course we intend to buy a piece of equipment in his name, for Alan's local hospital.

Thank you for buying this book, you've actively contributed to making that possible . . . and I hope you'll enjoy the stories too.

Julia Leberg

CONTENTS

FINE FEATHERS

11

SOMETHING OLD

25

SOMETHING NEW

35

SOMETHING BORROWED

49

SOMETHING BLUE

55

CLOBBERED

61

KITTED OUT

65

COSTUME DRAMA

77

FRILLS AND SPILLS

85

BLOOMERS

101

FITTING THE BILL

119

UNDRESS

133

FOLLIES

145

FINE
FEATHERS

MAUREEN LIPMAN

Ever Felt Red?

It was a red, circular skirt. Cut on the bias, my mother pointed out helpfully. In felt. All I knew was that I felt biassed towards having it. Mother thought it was a liability, i.e. it would have to be dry-cleaned, but I was twelve years old and had a Ph.D. in Advanced Whingeing. So finally, smugly, snugly it was mine.

Then came the search for the perfect sweater. In my mind's beady eye it was white with just a soupçon (had I known the word soupçon) of scarlet such as I'd once seen June Allyson sport in a skating sequence in some Saturday morning picture. Maybe if I got her outfit I'd get her husky voice to match?

After three successive Saturdays spent hissing in a changing room in C & A, I found it. It was white wool with a band of red figures waltzing round the welt. Gorgeous wasn't in

it – but before you can say 'It'll show every mark' – *I* was.

That evening, while the rest of the family watched *Dixon of Dock Green,* I gathered together the total ensemble and placed it upon my person. Red skirt, white sweater, snowy socks, shoes Tuxon'd scufflessly white – not by me, needless to say. To top it all I added a red and white ribbon to the crest of my perm. To do my family credit, no one actually *said* I looked like an animated barber's pole.

The party was at the weekend. Saturday. In school. The teacher had been specific about dress: 'Don't wear your best clothes, girls, there'll be lots of running around and some floor-games!' Sod that for a lark, thought Lipman, anxious to flash her felt at all costs. I climbed into it. Mentally I'd never been out of it. Peered into the mirror, pinched my cheeks, fiddled with my frizz, stuck out what should have been a chest, and, well pleased, sashayed, stiff with petticoats and pride, through the storm porch and out to the bus stop.

Strange to be in school at the weekend. Like some forbidden city. The cloakroom was abuzz with the 'ooh's' and 'aah's' of it all. I bided my timing till the last, then, Gypsy Rose Lee-like, flung off my good nap coat to reveal all. It was worth it – a gobsmacked silence followed by the 'ooh's' and 'aah's' to end them all.

'What? This?' I demurred. 'Oh, I've had it for aaaages – just never had the opportunity to wear it, so, y'know, thought I might as well ... You coming up or what?'

Flanked by friends all a-flutter, into the Assembly Hall, cleared of chairs for dancing and floor-games purposes. Teachers in mufti (giggle, giggle, point, snigger) calling over the rabble: 'Girls, girls, pleeese, now you can all make a circle and – QUIET PLEASE – settle DOWN!' – here she caught my eye, and then, swiftly, the rest of me – 'Ahem ... Could you all sit down' – here she definitely shot me a disdainful and slightly triumphant one – 'on the floor!' I drew myself up to my full 4 feet 8 inches, flared my pupils at the teacher, picked up my scarlet skirt, Vivien Leigh-style, and, with a thud, parquet met felt and felt met parquet. Frankly, my dear, I didn't *give* a damn!

It was halfway through Pass the Parcel that the penny finally dropped. 'Nelly the Elephant' had just been chorus-interruptus as she was saying

goodbye to the thingy, and a large girl in her mother's dirndl skirt from 3B was attacking the string round the paper with her teeth and pretending not to hear that the music had started again, when I felt the red drain out of my skirt and into my face.

'Don't wear your best clothes, there'll be floor-games' doesn't mean don't wear your best clothes, there'll be floor-games, you dull-brained twerp! It means don't wear your best clothes, there'll be some girls who don't *have* best clothes, so we don't want any showing off. Or up.

This thought, followed by an affirming glance round the circle, was enough to ruin not only the rest of the party but also the possibility of ever wearing my outfit care-lessly again. It sat in my wardrobe malevolently for a while until, out of sheer defiance, I grew two inches in as many months and in most directions. Dry-eyed, I acquiesced when it finally hit the bag of clothes for 'Poor Peggy, she's you-know-what-again, God help her' and I'm delighted to say I haven't given it a thought since. Not more than once a day, that is. For thirty years.

It was, I think, my first real understanding of what being spoiled meant, in more than one way, and it gave me a lifelong horror of over-dressing which, having just glanced through the photo-albums in search of an illustrative self-portrait, I can only say I seem to have conquered admirably.

JILLY COOPER

I remember with fondness my first black mini. I was walking down Bond Street in it at the end of the 60s when an American clapped his hands over his eyes and said: 'Oh my God, can they go any higher?' By today's standards the dress seems rather tame!

RONNIE BARKER

I have no special anecdote to go with this weird and wonderful picture of me at the age of seventeen, except that the black shirt and yellow tie with horses' heads is what I chose to wear for my first 'stage' photograph. I thought it was really theatrical and quite sexy. I was wearing this outfit when I smoked my first cigarette, met my first girl-friend, and went to my first audition. Sad to say, the black shirt has long disappeared – together with the black hair and the black eyebrows; all I have left are the freckles and the memories.

KATIE BOYLE

I still have vivid memories of my first long evening dress. Having always been a tomboy, happier in casual clothes, I felt certain I'd hate to be dolled up. Quite the contrary – my striding gait turned to a traipse, and I shushed the

wide skirt of paper taffeta as I went, because it made such a lovely, feminine sound. The puffed short sleeves and the neckline and skirt edged with self-shaded rosebuds spelt glamour, and I breathed in so that the tight bodice and nipped-in waist told as few tales as possible of my healthy appetite.

I think the memory of this dress is so vivid, because in it I crossed the barrier from tomboy to the realization that I was going to thoroughly enjoy being a girl!

JILL GASCOIGNE

I'd been asked to present something in the 'Laurence Olivier Awards Ceremony' which was to be broadcast live on television. I had been through my entire wardrobe for *Give Us A Clue* at least a dozen times – or so it seemed. Then I heard about 'One Night Stand'. Wonderful – you could hire a designer dress for one night. So off I set to the shop, armed with an idea for something in 'candy pink' which everyone tells me looks wonderful on telly and takes years off your age.

They had some pink dresses, but every one I tried on made me look like one of those dolls people used to put over toilet rolls to hide them – a somewhat coy generation, our mothers'! Gaye Brewn had said – if you have a pear shape and big hips (that's me! that's me!) you should always wear something fitted. Being shaped something like a cello, I've always thought I was at my best in something like a sack – even a bin liner. But I decided to take her advice – seeing as my mind and imagination had gone blank, as usual when faced with long rows of frocks.

I found it. Black, tight, low, with a wonderful fishnet sort of 'tail' or flounce at the bottom.

I hired it. And I wore it. My memories are thus – that although everyone told me in hushed tones that I looked absolutely 'stunning' (making me wonder if I had ever looked any good ever before) – I spent the entire evening holding my stomach in, not being able to eat, needing assistance in and out of the car, being terrified somebody would set the damn net flounces alight with a cigarette, and *dreading* going to the toilet. But you know, I think I'd do it again, just for the absolute sheer pleasure it was to take it off at the end of the evening and get into my pyjamas – which, incidently, are my very *favourite* outfit.

NEIL KINNOCK

Clothes and me have never got on very well – I just can't work up the interest. But back in the Fifties when I was in my teens things were different. Then the problem was that I couldn't work up the cash. But in 1958 I did get together dark brown loafers, plain red socks and jeans washed to the perfect pitch of blue. With a button-down collar shirt and a scuffed brown leather jerkin that had been left here by the American relative of a relative, I thought that I was the goods. The top wasn't very impressive I suppose. But from the waist down I could easily have been mistaken for James Dean.

GLENYS KINNOCK

In 1959 my mother finally conceded and took me to the shops to purchase the very first outfit which I considered suitable to qualify me to join the swingin' generation.

It consisted of a white lacey blouse with drawstring ribbons through the neck and sleeves. This was set off by a spectacular multi-coloured skirt underlayered with two or three paper nylon petticoats. They had to be soaked for hours in a solution of hot water and sugar to make them stick out and were a guaranteed attention-puller as I jived at the Saturday Scout's Hall hop. It gave a new meaning to 'Sweet Sixteen'.

My father thought it was hilarious. He said I looked like a lampshade on legs. And he didn't like the 'final touches'. Lipstick, powder and mascara were not thought to be 'nice' for a girl my age. Like my friends, therefore, I went to a telephone box to apply layers of make-up. The mirror was perfect. I rocked and rolled properly painted. My dad was happy. Bliss.

DAWN FRENCH

I would like to show you this picture of my brother, my mother and myself at a wedding about four hundred years ago. My 'fab gear' was pink. *Really* pink. Why do mothers publicly humiliate their children in this way?

SOMETHING OLD

EDWARD FOX

When I was seventeen years old I was working in the Kingston branch of Marks and Spencers as a trainee manager.

The accepted dress for gentlemen employees was a dark lounge suit.

One day I decided to wear an extremely elegant Prince of Wales check suit, left to me by my great-uncle. However, it did not conform to the dull strictures that applied to manager's dress in commercial trade.

On arriving at work I was summoned to the manager, Laurie Margaret, and asked, 'did I think I was cut out for this sort of work?' 'Had I ever considered going into the theatre?'

I replied in the negative to both questions, and was given my notice there and then.

KATHARINE
WHITEHORN

When I was a child I used to wear cast-offs, sometimes from my brother, which was peculiar, and sometimes bits of clothes of other relations and friends. My mother once cut a long stretch of tweed from the bottom of an adult coat and made it into a wraparound skirt for me, with immense pop fasteners. Never, never in my life will I forget the mortification and shame I felt when my brother, aged about 16, shrieking hilariously, ran round and round me unpopping the skirt outside the youth hostel in Graffham, Sussex. I have not been greatly given to modesty either then or since; but I have never felt more bare in spite of what I don't doubt was the sturdy seriousness of my knickers.

DEREK NIMMO

My first stage job, more than thirty years ago, was at the Hippodrome Theatre in Bolton. In those days a repertory contract specified that an actor had to provide, amongst other things, 'two good walking-out suits, a sports jacket and a dinner jacket'.

The plays were changed every week and the Lawrence Williamson Players (for it was they) couldn't afford to hire costumes. As even in those days I tended to give much the same performance irrespective of the play in which I was cast, it was obvious to me that it was important to effect a certain sartorial disguise to differentiate one part from another. But how?

Fortunately for me I formed a friendship with a local undertaker who seemed to have access to quantities of hardly-worn suits at a remarkably low price. I never enquired too closely from where they came; suffice it to say that they were still warm when I got them.

Amongst the garments that I managed to purchase (for half a crown) was a splendid, black smoking jacket with scarlet facings which I still besport on festive occasions.

DENIS NORDEN

According to this knowledgable friend of mine, 'The only thing that looks good in a plain brown jacket is a baked potato.' Intended as a direct criticism of the most cherished item in my wardrobe, the remark left me unperturbed because I have never even hoped to be what is generally understood by 'a trendy dresser'.

It could even be said that something within me actively resists trendiness. Back in the days when my group took David Niven as their role model, they would all wear a cravat knotted negligently round the neck and look incredibly elegant. On me, it just looked like I had a sore throat.

Further back still was the era when we thought the height of sophistication was wearing a camel-hair coat draped round the shoulders without putting one's arms through the sleeves. The only way I ever managed to bring that off was by remaining perfectly still. Whenever I attempted any forward motion, the coat would fall off one shoulder and trip me up.

Nor have I fared any better with Eighties fashions. My attempts to ape the recent fad for wearing one's jacket with the sleeves pushed up - the Rory Bremner look - failed miserably because my sleeves simply would not remain pushed up. I tried keeping them in position artificially by putting dots of Superglue just below each of my elbows, but if I ever pulled my jacket off absent-mindedly, the pain would make my eyes water. There are still little bald patches among the fine hairs on my forearm.

Consequently, I have never been under any illusions about where I would be positioned on one of those lists of the world's best-dressed men. It would be about three places below Yasser Arafat.

And that plain brown jacket did nothing to improve my position in the charts. But in spite of all the disparagement heaped upon it by those close to me - Frank Muir's contribution was 'Somewhere out there we must look for a shivering horse' - I really loved that jacket. A murky sort of brown it was, the kind of colour the water in a basin goes after you've peeled 2 kilos of

King Edwards in it, and the material was so heavy that if I had ever hung it on one of those wire-hangers that dry-cleaners thrust on you today, it would have bent the thing into the shape of twenty-past-eight.

As well as being heavy, the cloth was also quite singularly unyielding. 'Are you quite sure it isn't hardboard?' asked that same knowledgable friend the first time he fingered the lapels. I could understand his suspicions because in addition to having no sort of 'give', the jacket had another characteristic rarely associated with today's casual wear. As distinct from being 'shower-repellent' or 'moisture-resistant' or whatever it is that modern materials are supposed to be, that jacket somehow stored whatever rain fell on it. Sometimes it would remain squelchy to the touch for days afterwards.

But, as I say, I loved it. I always felt so secure when I had it on, though to this day I am not quite sure why. Probably it was because it took me back to my boyhood, when gents suitings always seemed to be made of stiff, heavy materials in plain, dingy colours. In those days, the only thing we could hope for in the way of a lightweight suit was a winter suit that had worn thin.

'Till it wilted I wore it, I'll always adore it' was that girl's valediction to her Alice Blue garment, but where my plain brown one was concerned nothing short of the thermo-nuclear could have put a wilt in it. The only reason I am not wearing it today is because I loaned it to my son when he was a student and, he claims, it was stolen by an industrial archaeologist he ran into.

It's possible, I suppose. Perhaps, though, I should have been alerted by what the lad said when he came asking to borrow it. 'Dad - I've got this Fancy Dress Party . . .'

SOMETHING
NEW

RAY COONEY

The salesman was surprised to say the least. I was in a department store in Detroit and it was just coming up to closing time. From the look on his face, I could see that he thought I was even more eccentric than he had been led to believe Englishmen were. I required a suit in a hurry. This, needless to say, was not unusual. However, what had thrown him off balance was that I wanted a suit to be both ill-fitting and drab.

My sartorial situation had arisen because the farce I had co-written with John Chapman, *Not Now Darling*, was playing in Detroit prior to opening in New York. I was directing the play and the leading role was in the hands of Norman Wisdom. The play had opened in Detroit the previous evening and I had called a rehearsal the following afternoon. I felt the main problem with the production was that Norman was 'indulging' himself and not giving the play the necessary drive, resulting in the performance running fifteen minutes longer than necessary. Norman disagreed. Finally having disagreed to such an extent that he said, 'If you think I am too slow, you play the part tonight.' As I had originally created the role, I thought it wasn't too bad an idea and so I agreed, hoping that Norman might realize that it was possible to be both sympathetic and swift. So it was arranged that Norman would sit at the back of the auidence while I appeared in the play. The other actors and actresses thought it was a splendid diversion to have the co-author and director performing with them, especially as there wasn't even time to have a rehearsal.

There was, course, the question of a costume. It was already 5.30pm and the performance was due to commence at 7.30pm.

I tried on the suit which Norman wore in the play but, not surprisingly, I couldn't even get into it. Hence the hasty rush to the department store. Having chosen a suit which was at least a size too large, I then offended the salesman even more by selecting a mis-matching shirt and tie. His eyes closed in anguish as I rolled the suit up and dumped it in a bag, explaining that I needed to look like a crumpled mess in about an hour's time.

Although I hadn't appeared in the play for several years, it all came back to me. It was a particularly responsive audience, with most of the laughs being where they should be – and the performance was fifteen minutes shorter.

The producer, Norman and I met up in Norman's dressing-room after the performance to discuss the situation. I felt I had shown that both the character and the play worked even better when the play's running time was reduced. The producer asked Norman for his opinion. After a long, thoughtful pause, Norman replied, 'I can't speak that fast.' We clearly had an impasse.

The producer's view was that either Norman or I should say farewell to the production before New York. I was just giving some thought as to what my view on this might be, when the producer gave me *his* view – and sacked me.

To the best of my knowledge there is to this day an ill-fitting drab suit with mis-matching tie and shirt hanging in the No. 1 dressing room of the Fisher Theater, Detroit.

SPIKE MILLIGAN

You ask if I remember an outfit – it was the worst suit I ever had, my demob suit, and I got it in Austria in 1946. The photograph of that occasion, alas, is stored at Pickfords along with the rest of my furniture and belongings until I can pay the rent. It is on the cover of my book *'Goodbye Soldier'* – I'm the one on the right!

HARRY SECOMBE

'That's the kind of outfit I want when I get out,' said Sgt. Terence Milligan nodding towards a passing Italian gentleman who happened to be wearing a shiny blue silk suit, dark glasses and a camel-hair coat slung across his shoulders. I agreed enthusiastically. 'Make a change from the stuff we're wearing now, Spike. When I get back into 'Civvy Street' I can sling this lot and get into a decent suit'.

Spike smiled enigmatically and stood up. 'Good luck son.' He picked up the bill from the saucer on the Naples cafe table. 'I shouldn't pay it if I were you,' he said, handing it to me.

I was still worrying about that enigmatic smile two weeks later as I shuffled along in the queue at the Aldershot Demob Centre. My first civvy suit for seven years was only a few yards away. In it I would conquer show business. When it came to my turn, a tailor ran a tape over me, tut-tutting at the state of my battledress and calling out figures to an assistant. The whole affair had a dream-like quality and I only woke up to reality when I found myself outside the Nissen hut with a cardboard box containing a chalk stripe suit, a pair of shoes, a couple of shirts and a tie, an overcoat of outrageous blue material and a pork pie hat. In fact, not exactly what was needed to break into the West End – I'd have trouble breaking into the West End of Swansea. It was then I began to realise the meaning of Milligan's enigmatic smile.

However, when I finally arrived home at 48 Hazel Road, Swansea, things looked different. With a bit of help from my mother and my sister, Carol, the suit didn't look too bad. The trouble was that I didn't look right in it. I kept swinging my arms when I walked and the considerable difference in weight between my Army boots and the much lighter pair of shoes I had been issued with induced in me a high-stepping gait not unlike that of an American cheer leader.

When I first ventured out to meet some of my mates, I decided , in view of

my deep Mediterranean tan, to try to look like the smart Italian Spike and I had envied. I borrowed a pair of clip-on sunglasses from Carol, slung my new blue coat over my shoulders and set off up Hazel Road. We hadn't lived there long before I left for North Africa in November 1942 but even so I had a small reputation for eccentricity.

It was a pretty overcast day and at first I had difficulty in seeing where I was going, and then a strong breeze blew up from the sea front. Now it's not an easy job to keep control of an overcoat in the wind if you happen to have your arms out of the sleeves. I wrestled with the damned thing until I got almost to the bottom of the road where I walked into a lamp post. At least, I thought to myself as I walked into the pub, I'm out of uniform. 'Hello lads,' I called out to Danny Williams, Josh Jones, Vic Kelly and Alan Gaukroger. They turned from the bar, each one identical in chalk stripe suits. 'Join the club, mate,' said Danny.

That night, after I had collected the first beer stains on my new suit, we all decided to go to the Mumbles Pier where there was a dance on. We marched together – it was difficult to walk out of step in those days – to the Mumbles railway and boarded the train. Once inside the dance hall it was more beer all round and I plucked up enough Dutch courage to ask a dark haired girl, who happened to look very Italian, for a dance. I was then in my 'Canadian' phase and for a moment or two I fooled her. Then she noticed the suit I was wearing and she knew I could not be the Canadian officer I pretended to be. However, by the end of the second dance I had arranged to meet her the following evening. Two years later we were married. I wore a grey bird's eye suit for the wedding because, by that time, the chalk stripe demob suit had gone.

One morning a year previously I had crept out of the flat I shared with Spike and Norman Vaughan in Notting Hill Gate with a bundle under my arm. I was very strapped for cash at the time and there was a second-hand clothes dealer in a back street nearby who'd buy anything. I sold him the bundle under my arm for 35 shillings. Ten shillings of that was for my demob suit, the rest was for Milligan's overcoat. But that's another story.

MICHAEL ASPEL

When I was a teenager we were, so far as fashion was concerned, simply small replicas of our elders. At that time clothes rationing was still in effect. For each garment, the draper's scissors snipped away at your little brown booklet. I still remember my first pair of long trousers. I've never been exactly mighty in the thigh, so that to get a pair of trousers to fit around the middle and reach the ankle was a problem. They only seemed to make them for people who were built to standard proportions. I tried on many pairs, all of dreadful quality – a cheap coarse flannel – we couldn't afford worsted, even with my school grant. If they reached my shoes, the crutch was just above my knee. If they fitted around the loins, then you could see the tops of my socks.

Eventually we compromised, and settled for a pair that didn't fit anywhere. But I was thrilled. They were my first pair of long trousers, a sign of manhood, and if I stuck my bottom out and bent my knees slightly, they wouldn't look too bad.

Sometime later I bought a jacket in a sale. It had survived several sales, I think. It was double-breasted and sky blue. People covered their eyes and reeled back when I approached. I wore it for the Boat Race that year and it never occurred to me to feel incongruous shouting 'Come on, Oxford', in my coat of shimmering pale blue. Oddly enough, the BBC commentator must have been colour-blind too, because he came up to me and asked me if I was an Oxford supporter. I said of course, and he said would I like to come along after the race and talk into his microphone. Unfortunately, I was swept away by the crowd and so missed my chance of a broadcasting debut at the age of fourteen.

LIBBY PURVES

I shall never forget my tight green baize miniskirt and mock-suedette jerkin with football buttons. I made the outfit myself. I was fifteen (1965). I looked absolutely dreadful. Especially with my white plastic cutaway Courèges boots and shiny vinyl (PVC) John Lennon peaked cap.

PAUL McCARTNEY

My first pair of long trousers. They were grey flannel and had been bought for me by my Dad. The problem was that they were too wide at the bottom for the fashion at the time which was 16 inches top whack! Fortunately, however, I had a friend by the name of Ian James (from the Dingle) who suggested that we bunk out of school at lunch-time with the offending articles and have them altered by a local tailor that afternoon. I arrived back at school just before 4 o'clock sporting trousers which were now an acceptable 14 inches and very wearable indeed!

At home that evening when my father enquired suspiciously 'Are those the same trousers I bought you?' I was able to look into his eye with great honesty and say 'Yes Dad'. . . .

CYRIL SMITH

I remember my first
Grammar School blazer.
It came from a
jumble sale -
all my Mum
could afford,
but I was mighty
proud to wear it.

SOMETHING
BORROWED

ROBERT MORLEY

One of the more bizarre theatrical engagements in my youth was a season at the Cambridge Festival Theatre, presided over by a rather eccentric millionaire, Terence Gray, who lived nearby in a house called Gog and Magog. It made a nice change from touring in *Is Your Honeymoon Really Necessary?* and *Almost a Honeymoon*. We offered Greek tragedy by Euripides, Latin comedy by Terence, and *Gustavus Vasa* by Strindberg. Terence Gray who had a rather pronounced stutter, was chary of verbal instructions but communicated his views on our performance by hand-written and largely indecipherable notes. Undergraduates, as is the custom in university enclaves, preferred to slope off to the cinema. Terence printed a programme which could be read when the houselights dimmed by holding it aloft, aimed at the floats. He was immensely proud of the most advanced lighting equipment in Britain.

The acting was a shade indiscriminate. I played the name part in *Gustavus* and was judged a trifle young to go hatless. Terence solved the problem by fitting me out with an Ascot hat in straw with a poppy. His ex-wife had apparently worn it and left it behind along with him when she walked out. I made my entrance through the auditorium and climbed on to the stage before delivering my first line to an attendant courtier. 'Do you think,' I enquired, 'we have been recognised?' For once I had them rolling in the aisles.

When we came to Euripides, Terence fitted us all out in masks made of sorbo sponge. A loyal aunt came to watch. 'I loved it, of course,' she told me, 'but was bothered by the mask you wore. Do you know, it looked as if it was made of sorbo sponge from where I sat. I don't believe the Greeks had sorbo sponge in those days.'

MILES KINGTON

I went to school in Scotland, to a place where you had to wear a kilt on Sundays. Coming from south of the border as I did, this seemed a silly thing to do and I didn't realize until I'd been wearing the thing for a year or two that I actually quite enjoyed it and even preferred it in some ways to the trouser. Women will know what I'm talking about. They have the freedom to pass at will from trousers and skirt and back again, via the culotte, but generally the only men who know the delights of flowing fabric round the knees are transvestites and Scots.

For the benefit of any reader who is not female, transvestite or Scottish (and even there we have to remember that most Scots never wear a kilt), I can reveal that the kilt is light, does not get soaking when you are walking through long grass, is pleasantly tactile when brushing against the thighs, allows you to go to the lavatory instantly and swings like mad when you are dancing. It feels nice and looks quite dashing. You can wear nothing underneath it if you like and if you want to freeze to death, but then the Scots have had a lot of self-defeating customs in the past, such as putting salt on porridge, adding lemonade to whisky and believing they are going to win the World Cup. They only succeed in making things worse.

It would never have occurred to me to wear the thing south of the border, so I was quite surprised when my brother Stewart, younger than me and still a teenager, asked if he could borrow it to go on holiday.

'Where are you going?'

'Africa.'

'*Africa?* It will be too hot for a kilt in Africa.'

'I don't want it for wearing, idiot elder brother. I want it for hitching.'

Did you know this? I didn't. Apparently it is dead cinch to get a lift on the Continent if you wear a kilt. Half the motorists stop because they think you're a girl and the other half because they are intrigued, and you get twice the place in half the time. But I've always been the boring sort of safe elder

brother who never goes hitching and Stewart is the kind of interesting younger brother who does. Anyway, he and his friend who also had a kilt went off hitching to Africa and got there in record time, this being in the days before Rangers supporters got the club the rough sort of reputation that Rangers players get for it nowadays.

When he got back, he looked slightly crestfallen. He had left the kilt behind in Morocco. He had had to leave in a hurry, apparently, because it was a time of warlike activity against freedom fighters and they were suspected of being spies. But to leave my kilt behind . . .!

'I'm going back next year,' he said. 'I'll get it then.'

He went back next year. What happened then was that he was put in jail. They still had him on the records as a suspected spy and it was only after some time, which he spent learning chess from his cell-mate (a Yugoslav deserter from the Foreign Legion), that he was released and unceremoniously bundled out of the country, again without my kilt.

That was in 1963. If you should happen to be in Morocco soon, and you are offered for sale in the market a curiously wrought blue, green and black rug with holes, buckles and fastenings in it, please buy it and bring it back to me. I miss it.

SOMETHING BLUE

IVOR DANVERS

I began my theatrical career at an early age, and one of the first parts I was asked to play was Prince Arthur, brother of the later Henry VIII, in a play called *The Patched Cloak*, at the Boltons Theatre in Kensington, now sadly no more. It was an exciting play, and rehearsals went well until the full dress parade on stage. Most of my costume was fine, and I thought I cut a fine, princely figure from the waist up. But the tights were the problem. They were made of silk, very fine, and I was assured by the Wardrobe Mistress they had been worn previously by Laurence Olivier in the film *Hamlet*. I was just fifteen at the time, and rather weedy. Someone had mentioned the word 'jockstrap' to me, but, as I was earning a pittance, it seemed like an unnecessary expense, so I thought I would make do with my underpants.

However, the effect was rather less than satisfactory. Instead of a nice clean line, my mid-area looked, to coin a phrase, like a bagful of spanners. I decided to grasp the nettle and do away with my underpants altogether. The result looked better at the back, but rather mind-boggling infront. Still, I was an actor, I thought, and above such petty modesty. I walked on to the stage for costume inspection, trying to look as princely as possible. Unfortunately, the effect of the bright lights made my tights look practically transparent, so that I gave the impression of being a Christmas tree from the waist up, and stark naked from the waist down.

I heard the director and designer murmuring for a few moments in the stalls, while I stood there regally, trying to look like Prince Arthur about to wed Catharine of Aragon. But then I distinctly heard the director whisper, 'For God's sake, take that poor little bugger away, and cover him up,' followed by a titter from someone.

I was eventually kitted out satisfactorily, but the memory haunts me still.

Ivor Danvers trying to look regal

GYLES BRANDRETH

I'm not sure what it was called, but it looked horrific and it was hell to wear. I only bought mine because I knew Nicholas Parsons already had one. His was no better fit than mine - as we both discovered halfway through the night.

I take it you've guessed what I'm on about. It isn't easy to put delicately, but I'll try. The garment I'm bringing out of my closet for you consisted of an elastic belt with, hanging from it, a long rubber tube. Worn beneath one's trousers, it was designed as the ultimate portaloo, a convenience you can actually wear. In short an appliance that enables you to perform anywhere at any time.

I was wearing mine (and Nicholas was wearing his) in the same place on the same night because we were both taking part in an unusual charity marathon: a joint assault on the world record for the longest-ever after-dinner speech. We had to speak non-stop, without hesitation or deviation, not for just a minute but for just on eleven hours. And the rules of the *Guinness Book of Records* required that an after-dinner speech take place after dinner, which meant talking through the night. In adjoining rooms at the Hyde Park Hotel in London we each rose at 9 pm knowing that we couldn't honourably sit down until 8 o'clock the following morning, but at least secure in the knowledge that if nature called we could answer that call without interrupting the flow - if you see what I mean. (I am trying to put this nicely, I really am.)

When it comes to clothes there's a golden rule that on key occasions you shouldn't wear something you've not worn before. Don't wear a brand-new suit to that crucial interview; wear a good suit but one you know. Unfortunately, neither Nicholas nor I heeded this golden rule. We had no dry run. (This really isn't an easy story to tell, is it?)

At 8 pm on the dot we were all strapped up and ready for action. By midnight we were both in full swing and, because long-distance speaking is thirsty work and we were both equipped with the ultimate security blanket, we were blithely taking regular and hefty sips of water. By 2 am we'd both been speaking for six hours and I for one was beginning to feel the need for a little light relief - relieving yourself in front of a hundred dinner-jacketed charity supporters, even if they don't know you are doing it, calls for courage - I took a final swig of water and glanced to the ground. There, trailing from my trouser leg, was a long, a very long, rubber tube. Plunging my hands into my pockets I groped hopefully, but it was too late. The appliance had slipped its mooring and was gently descending my inside leg and making its snakelike way out into the open.

How I survived the next five hours without inflicting permanent personal injury I'll never know - but I managed. And so did Nicholas. As it turned out, he had lost his within minutes of me losing mine, and at the end of our eleven hour ordeal we both made our ways into the *Guinness Book of Records* and the Gents at exactly the same moment. Since Mafeking I don't believe there's been a relief like it.

Andrew Festing's painting of "The Longest-Ever
After-Dinner Speech" which was unveiled at
Buckingham Palace on 18th November 1982.
The painting commemorates Gyles Brandreth's
12½ hour speech given in aid of the National
Playing Fields Association.

UNA STUBBS

The costume I remember most was in the *Folies Bergère* (Piccadilly). We dancers were part of the 'Dresden Tableau' for the 'Ganjon Brothers and Inanita' adagio act. For 10 mins – or was it 10 hours? – we stood motionless, dressed in American cloth (pre-plastic) crinolines and a complete rubber all-in-one mask and wigs pulled over our faces and heads like a giant ornate condom with 3 minute holes for eyes and mouth, as it was one of the rare nude productions on in London in those days. We were able to stop ourselves fainting from suffocation by watching the men in the audience 'fidgiting' at the sight of the nudes also in the tableau.

CLOBBERED

GEORGE COLE

The only costume I remember with no pleasure at all is an animal skin when I played a hyena in *Where the Rainbow Ends.* I was only fourteen, very small, and the skin was made for somebody a bit more robust. I couldn't see out of the eye-holes and kept bumping into other 'animals', with the result that I got badly knocked about by the Wolves!

ALAN AYCKBOURN

I was once in a production of *Mademoiselle Jaire* by Ghelderode when an acting ASM [Assistant Stage Manager] of seventeen or so, and was foolish enough to criticize the costume designer. I was cast, among other parts, as an angel in a carnival scene. The designer provided me with an all-in-one garment made of two sets of long johns sewn together, a huge padded stomach, a ten-foot orange tail that trailed behind, a papier maché mask with a two-foot nose, and an archbishop's mitre two sizes too small for me.

I spent a miserable two weeks trying to balance the hat whilst others collided with my stomach, stood on my feet, trod on my tail or inadvertently flattened my nose.

I am very nice to costume designers even today.

KITTED OUT

CLAIRE RAYNER

Metamorphosis, that was the name of the game; in a matter of ten minutes or so, in the privacy of my small bedroom in the Royal Northern Hospital's Nurses' Home, I would be changed from an ordinary rather gawky girl into a Fount of All Wisdom, an Angel of Mercy, a rather cheeky female who Knew How to Look After Herself, and who would therefore attract leering glances and suggestive chat-up lines from stupid men who were as unattractive as they were witless – as I say, metamorphosis. I was to put on my uniform for the first time.

And heavens, what a concoction of calico and cambric it was! But, stockings and shoes first; thick black lisle stockings ('Never nylon, Nurse,' Sister Tutor said crisply. 'It creates static electricity which could cause explosions and fires around volatile substances used for anaesthesia and so forth, and anyway they look too – hurrumph – interesting'), and great clod-hopping black lace-ups that made your feet hurt just to look at them. Stockings held up by suspenders, of course – this was the early 1950s, and who'd ever imagined such things as tights? – which constantly separated themselves from your girdle with a loud ping, and which left lots of bare thigh above the stocking tops to be rubbed by the heavy calico of the dress.

Ye gods, that dress! Thick, heavy, striped in pale blue and white, and made up as an exact copy of a parlour maid's uniform circa 1880. Buttoned down the bodice with thick rubber buttons which were supposed to survive regular laundering well (they didn't) and with a deep placket at the left-hand side for some unknown purpose (I never managed to work it out), and three deep tucks taken in the mid-calf length skirt. Mid-calf at a time when most people wore skirts just below the knee! Dowdy wasn't the word for it.

The dress had long sleeves, which had to be rolled up over the elbows for work, with starched white frills set over the rolled-up part, so that they looked neat. When we went to meals or lectures or to be bullied by Matron, the sleeves were rolled down, the frills tucked away into the capacious hip

pocket of the dress, and stiff starched deep white cuffs were set over the sleeve ends. These cuffs were fastened with heavy metal cufflinks, and matched the collar of the dress. This was separate, again so heavily starched and so stiff it looked and felt like glossy cardboard (and cut into a soft neck cruelly), and was held in place at the back with a back stud and in front with – guess what? – a front stud. We bought these at Woolworths at a penny each (old money) and lost them with heartbreaking frequency and great inconvenience. Some of us had a stock of them for our own use and for lending to desperate friends who were not so provident. Finally, into the breast pocket of the dress went a pair of scissors, a pencil, and a pocket watch (wrist watches were *verboten* to us first years), and that was *all*. God help you if Sister caught you with any other items there.

So far, so good. Now the apron. A sheet of crackling white starch, fastened at the waist at the back with a large safety-pin (the only thing you could do to give the outfit any style at all was to pinch in the waist as hard as you could), and pinned at the front with special tabs that attached them to the dress just above the boobs. We did not have over-the-shoulder straps, for which we were deeply grateful. They looked even more parlour-maidish, we thought. Over this went a wide white belt, again of heavily starched cambric, and from the moment we put on these white belts we yearned for the day when they would be exchanged for a striped one which happened at the end of your first year when you'd passed your Primary State exam, and later a black petersham belt fastened with an ornate silver buckle, which happened when you reached the heady heights of three years of completed training and success at the Final State exam. But I digress. Back to that first time.

Last of all came the cap, and this was a real horror. We wore butterflies; staff nurses wore pretty concoctions of lace frills attached to a Sister Dora cap – the sort of simple fold-over job so familiar from so many advertisements for lavatory paper (you can use the image of a uniformed nurse to sell the most *disgusting* things), and sisters wore classic veils. Great white sheets of starched lawn that floated on the air and made the old battleaxes look positively ethereal and saintly. Huh! They should have known those ladies as well as we juniors did. But again, I digress. Let me initiate you into the hell of making up a butterfly cap.

It started as a starched oblong of white cambric. This had to be folded, pleated and tweaked, while the centre of one short side was pinned to your bed or to your knee, into a flyaway thing that perched on top of your head very precariously held by a couple of hair grips, while the rest flew away behind in a flap of pleats and curves and side wings. Really very pretty, if cumbersome, and it took at least five minutes to make up a clean one. Sometimes you made such a bish of it you had to discard it and try another and then the laundry complained at how much you sent them. And they were the devil to wear, having a great tendency to slip to the back of your head (especially curly heads like mine) and to come adrift. Also, you had to be careful when you sat in a high-backed chair; I have to tell you that to this very day when I am extra tired and sit in such a chair and go to lean back, I automatically put my hand behind my head to flip up the remembered tails of my butterfly cap. And it's almost thirty-five years since I wore one of the wretched things!

As I say, it was a hell of an outfit to climb into. It was hot and scratchy in summer, cumbersome yet unwarming in winter, even when surmounted by a short navy cloth cloak lined in scarlet flannel and tied in place with crossed-over scarlet straps. We called them bum freezers, because they did so little for that sadly neglected portion of our anatomies, and used them to rub up our dusty shoes.

The whole uniform was also hell to work in; when you bent over a bed to hoist up a patient, the resulting expanse of white thigh above stocking tops brought whistles from the rest of the men and a reprimand from Sister. When you got hot and sweated, the fabric frankly reeked no matter how careful you were with deodorants, and if a patient bled on you - or worse - getting changed took ages. Today's nurses in their simple drip-dry dresses or trouser suits and chuckaway ready-made paper caps have a much easier time of it.

And yet, you know, when I look at the photographs I think - you did look rather divine in that gear, didn't you? Whatever you may have thought at the time . . .

CLEMENT FREUD

The chef's clerk said, 'And you getta your clothes ata Denny's in Old Compton Strada.' Those were the days when one did what one was told: I went and bought 2 pairs of blue check trousers, 4 cooks jackets, 2 hats. The latter, 15 inches tall, made of linen and being new, were unstarched. For the first two weeks of my working life I was the apprentice cook whose tall white hat rested on his left shoulder. The other apprentices came from families of chefs, and starched headgear had been put down for them at birth. There is much to be said for staying in the family profession . . . though possibly not my family's profession.

LARRY

My first army uniform is the outfit I most remember – a British Army blouse with smarter Canadian Army trousers – two different shades of khaki, and all this topped off by the highly unfashionable Ordinary Rank beret of that time. I suffered about three weeks feeling a complete clot until, by some wheeler dealing, I managed to acquire a Canadian blouse to match the trousers plus an officer's beret nicked on a pub outing.

It was around this time – mid 1946 – that ORs were first permitted to wear a collar and tie. So, strolling around Bodbrooke Camp (Royal Warwicks) in bad light, I was often taken for an officer and got saluted.

I soon ended up on a charge of impersonating an officer, received seven days Confined to Barracks and was ordered to 'unsmarten up'.

No problem this. A quick roll in the mud outside hut 29, a woodbine drooping from the lips, and hands in pockets – I looked every inch the real thing. The British Army, Ordinary Rank, 1946 vintage.

BROWNISH KHAKI

GREENISH KHAKI

DAVID JACOBS

HMS *Royal Arthur* turned out to be a converted holiday camp, where we were lodged in cosy chalets instead of draughty barrack rooms and slept on deep, deep mattresses instead of hammocks. Three days after our arrival we each got a hammock and a thin 'biscuit' to line it. These we lashed and stowed in seamanlike fashion each morning and unrolled each night. But we still slept on the mattresses. We were also issued with uniforms at the same time, thus ending a situation that I had been finding increasingly irritating and depressing.

I never cease being amazed at the docility or perversity with which – come war, fire or famine – we sort ourselves into class groups, or float into them from force of habit. In the three days before we got our uniforms, the draft of ordinary young civilians destined to become ordinary young seamen meticulously graded itself, without any outside help or instruction, into a series of isolated cliques in strict conformity with each individual's accent, eating habits, and relative costs of suits, linen and footwear. Sports jackets in one group, flannel shirts in another; hound's tooth sniffing defensively at herring-bone; handkerchief-in-sleeve-cuff drifting quietly away from handkerchief-in-breast-pocket; in the distance blue serge and no handkerchief at all. The 'gentlemen' feigned unawareness of the 'yobbos'; the 'yoicks' glared under their eyebrows at the 'toffs'. And they say it is women who are clothes-conscious!

I do not suggest it was either the 'toffs' or the 'yobbos' who made the first move towards segregation. I'm quite sure it was instinctive and sheeplike on all sides. It would have been comical if it had not been so miserably stupid. Fortunately, with the issue of uniforms and the disappearance of most of the class and income labels that we display in civilian life, we all became the best of friends, helping each other into the unfamiliar and complicated naval rig and strutting up and down like a covey of mannequins. Kitting-up and some square-bashing knocked us into a common pattern and it was not until a fortnight later, when we moved on to the seamanship course on H.M.S. *Ganges,* at Shotley Barracks, Ipswich, that individual identities began to emerge again. Then the sheep were separated from the goats, the men from the boys, the sailors from the lubbers.

JACK ROSENTHAL

I went from being Just William to Lieutenant-Colonel Rosenthal of the Royal Canadian Mounted Police almost overnight.

I'd been in my Just William phase for a long time – virtually ever since my Flash Gordon and The Clay Men phase, really (I'd been a Clay Man) – and it was beginning to pall.

To be Just William I had to race home from school each day, wolf down the slice of bread and jam that stopped you dying of starvation till tea was ready, and get into my uniform. This entailed smearing all excess jam round my face, roughing up my hair, pulling one sock down to the ankle and the other half-way down in careful wrinkles, ramming my tie under my ear, yanking my trouser-pockets inside out, tugging one side of my jacket off-the-shoulder and trudging out into the street.

There I'd rub a few daubs of mud on my knees, tread in the puddles and shuffle up and down the gutter waiting for an adventure.

Outfit-wise, I didn't look all that different from when I *wasn't* being Just William, and adventures were a bit thin-on-the-ground in our gutter. So I hung up my catapult and accepted a commission in the Mounties.

I got the idea in the first place when I noticed my red blazer at the back of the wardrobe. It was a couple of years old now but hardly worn on the grounds that it was too big for me and made me look a twerp. Now it was too *small* for me and made me look a *bigger* twerp.

But that was as a mere *boy*. As a Mountie, I was going to look terrific.

The nearest thing to a Mounties' hat that I could think of was a Scout hat, so I joined the Scouts. Unfortunately this was post-war Austerity Britain and Scout-hats were high on the list of nationwide shortages. True to the Scout motto 'Be Prepared', however, I rummaged in a cupboard and found an old, battered Scout hat under a pile of ropes and banners. And stole it.

Since the red blazer obviously didn't button up to the neck like a proper tunic, I reckoned a white shirt and black tie would do instead – especially for

Jack Rosenthal

an officer. I didn't have any ties apart from my school one, but luckily, the pal who was being Henry when I was being Just William gave me a blue one. Fine. Red, white and blue.

I fastened one belt round my waist with a gun and holster tied to it, and another across my chest like a Sam Browne. (I fastened it with the snake buckle at the back so's it wouldn't be noticed.)

So far, so good.

It was only while pulling on my wellingtons (i.e. riding boots) that I realized there was something missing apart from a horse.

Trousers.

Trousers with a *stripe* down them.

The only ones I could think of that could reasonably double as Mounties' trousers were bandsmen's ones. That Sunday I sat on the grass in front of the bandstand, pretending to look ecstatic while the band blasted Souza and my ear-drums all over Alkincoats Park. When they finally wheezed into silence, I politely asked if any of them had a pair of trousers they didn't need any more. They shook the spit out of their trumpets and told me to bugger off.

I finally solved the problem by wearing my pyjama trousers. True, they had *several* stripes instead of *one* and I was too embarrassed to leave my bedroom in them ... but when I locked the door, and stood on the bed from where I could see myself in the wardrobe mirror, full-length and in full regalia, I was the nearest thing to a Mountie I'd ever seen. Especially round our way.

It's only *after* childhood that you need glasses to see yourself as you are

COSTUME
DRAMA

NIGEL HAWTHORNE

I was dressing for the *Mapp and Lucia* series at London Weekend Television. My strawberry toupée was pinned into position, my face pinked, my fingernails buffed and I was dressed in a sort of lavender thing with a big bow, when the fire alarm went. An extremely officious person told us that we would have to descend immediately to the street via the fire escape as this was a fire drill exercise.

There was no way I was going to go down to the street looking like that. With the officious person glaring I removed every vestage of 'Georgie', put on my own clothes and joined the others standing down below.

I suppose if it had been a real fire I might have thought differently.

FRANK MIDDLEMASS

It was at Bristol Old Vic that I played a character called Utnapishtin in a piece by Durrenmatt called *An Angel Comes to Babylon* or something. It's all so long ago that the details are vague in my mind. Anyhow, this old gentleman was supposed to be over a hundred – a sort of wise man, guru, magician or what have you. I wore a long blue silk robe and a skull-cap and I had a long, straggly beard. I looked rather like the Honourable Mr Wong on a night out.

It occurred to me that the whole effect would be much enhanced by long Chinese finger-nails and these I resourcefully made for myself from those little plastic pellets which used to contain petrol for refilling cigarette lighters in those far-off days. Every night I would stick these damn things on the ends of my fingers and they looked magnificent, though I say it as shouldn't.

What I hadn't realized was that once I had them glued on I was a man who had lost the use of his hands. I couldn't open a door, couldn't do up a button, and consequently couldn't go to the loo. Couldn't do *anything*. The run of the play was to me a total nightmare.

The moral of this story is: Beware of over-elaboration in a role, and when you've had a thoroughly bad idea don't be pig-headed enough to stick with it.

PAUL EDDINGTON

In 1966 I did a musical called *Jorrocks.* In it I had to change, at lightning speed, from a Victorian gentleman to a Turkish Pasha. It took about twenty seconds.

Audiences are so used to cutting from one scene to another on TV that no one thought this was particularly remarkable until one night when my dressers and I fumbled something and I reappeared on stage still doing something up.

The audience must have realized what a feat it was and burst into a round of applause!

I fumbled something every night after that!

BARRY CRYER

Engraved on my heart, just below 'Skegness is so bracing', is the memory of the suit I wore on my first appearance in Variety, in nineteen hundred and typing error. The scene was the Royalty Theatre, Chester, and I was in my Terry Thomas phase.

I feel I should explain. The comedian and film actor was (and still is) an idol of mine and I decided to emulate him. Blithely ignoring the grave handicap of a Leeds accent as thick as last Thursday's Yorkshire pudding, I acquired a grey suit, a pearl waistcoat, a cigarette holder and (this is where the story really begins) an artificial pink carnation.

Parading backstage in this pathetic facsimile of the urbane Thomas, I was accosted by the stage manager – a man who resembled nobody so much as an ugly Kruschev. He enquired as to whether my carnation was 'fire-proofed', a term with which I was unfamiliar. Upon my reply that I had no idea, he produced a cigarette lighter and promptly set fire to it. The carnation, that is.

The ensuing sartorial inferno led to a frantic search for Chester's invisible mender. That night I made a shaky theatrical debut, with a rendition of Terry Thomas' act that required subtitles, and a left lapel that appeared to have had major heart surgery.

There *is* a happy ending. Some years later, the entire suit was destroyed by fire.

Barry Cryer, News at Ten, Chester.

JUNE WHITFIELD

It was the dress rehearsal of the pantomime in which I was playing 'Fairy Sweetcorn' and my exquisite fairy dress was ready in the dressing-room with my fairy wand, wings, head-dress, jewels and shoes – *but* – the very important petticoat which gave the dress its 'line' was missing!

'Oh, it's in the main wardrobe,' said one. 'Isn't it in your room?' was the answer from the main wardrobe. I tried not to panic but time was running short – the first night was the next night and I was a totally limp-looking fairy, tripping over my longer than usual trailing chiffon.

Then I remembered 'Mother's trunk' at home in the attic, full of props and 'useful clothes' which she had collected during the years when she took part in many amateur productions.

I rummaged through the trunk, and there, beneath Mary Queen of Scots' head-dress, fur tippets and fans, was a full-length calico petticoat with a frill round the bottom – almost identical to the missing one. The day was saved, and 'Fairy Sweetcorn' was able to appear on the first night of the pantomime suitably dressed – thanks to my dear departed Mum's petticoat.

PATRICK MOORE

I do have vivid memories of one 'costume'. The episode took place when I was living at East Grinstead in Sussex, so it must have been *circa* 1960. The local society put on a Christmas pantomime and, as usual, I played the Demon King (at my present home in Selsey, I still do; I specialize in demons).

On this occasion we were asked to take the show to a children's hospital near Tunbridge Wells. We did so. Obviously I drove over. We put on the show; I was attired in a totally green make-up, with sinister cloak and all the usual demonic trappings.

The rest of the cast had come by coach; I had driven on my own. I was about the last to leave, and as the coach drew out I remembered that my de-makeup kit and gear were in it. No matter; nobody was going to see me if I drove home for fifteen miles in my own car dressed as a demon.

The car wouldn't start!

Have you ever had to do a bus journey from one town to another dressed as a demon? People gave me *very* odd looks indeed. One woman got on the bus at Withyham, gave a shrill scream and got off again. One old boy asked if I were starting a new fashion; I assured him that it was the new Tunbridge Wells spirit, but I doubt if he believed me.

I finally got off the bus just before East Grinstead – I lived down a lane a mile out of the town – and met two late-night revellers clearly on their way home from the pub. I will never forget the looks on their faces. I never found out who they were, but I rather imagine that for the rest of their lives they were strict teatotalers!

FRILLS
AND
SPILLS

FRANK MUIR

And then there is the question of having your clothes pressed. I was once badly caught out. I had hurled a rain-soaked dinner-jacket into the bottom of a cupboard to be taken to the dry-cleaners later, retrieved it the following morning in a fearful state of crumpledom and whisked it up to the 24-hour clean and press emporium in Virginia Water only to find that their presser (the machine not the operator) had blown a gasket and was useless - and I had a dinner to speak at that evening.

The misery of wearing borrowed finery, too small, which made me look like a black-clad Norman Wisdom, was such that I could not sleep that night for wondering whether there was not a more satisfactory, more reliable, method of pressing clothes than having to take them to a shop and wait. Pressing the stuff perhaps *in situ*, or on the hoof.

And the answer came. As I lay in bed, a new and perfectly feasible way of pressing suits sprang to mind.

I used the idea later in a 'My Word' story on the wireless and here it is in print.

I *still* think it would work . . .

Let us now praise famous men, and the fathers that begat us
Ecclesiasticus xliv. 1

I answered the front door one evening and there stood a thinnish, faintly familiar figure.

'Yes?' I said.

'It's me!' said the figure. 'Nicholas. Nicholas Menon. Husband of Carol. Your vicar.'

I peered. 'So it is! Come in, old friend!'

I persuaded him to accept a glass of herbal mixture - the juice of juniper berries, distilled, with ice and lemon and not too much tonic - and brought

the conversation round to the change in his appearance.

'You used to be thick, Nick,' I said, groping for tactful words. 'But you've lost a lot of weight. You're now, how can I put it, a slicker vicar. What pared away the pounds? A diet? Dietary biscuits? A cellular wafer?'

'A glandular fever. But herein lies my problem. My clothes are now four sizes too large and I am to officiate at a wedding tomorrow.'

'As indeed I know,' I answered warmly. 'The *Staines and Egham News* is my bible. Sunninghill Parish Church. Morning-suits, marquee among the rhododendrons and the cream of the *Tatler's* photographic staff.'

'Even so,' he said. 'Now, I have found one suit that fits me, a clerical grey number from my student days which was lagging the church boiler, and I have taken it to the cleaners in Virginia Water. They assure me that it will be ready for collection just before I have to set out for the wedding tomorrow.'

'Well, that should do the trick, Nick.' I replied. 'Wherein lies your problem?'

'The manager of the cleaners has just telephoned to say that his pressing machine has expired in a cloud of steam. My suit will be cleaned, spun in a drum until dry, but, alas, not pressed.'

'Ah!' I said. 'So you either officiate tomorrow looking like Stan Laurel wearing Oliver Hardy's suit, or wearing a suit straight out of the spin-dryer, wrinkled like a walnut.'

'There seems no other choice.'

I mixed us another half-litre of herbal comfort.

'Timings?' I asked.

'Collect suit, 2.30. Drive back to Thorpe Vicarage and change at great speed. Arrive at the church at 2.50. I can just do the journey in 16 minutes - Carol timed me yesterday with the kitchen plinger.'

I am a firm believer in Lateral Thinking in problems like these. So I assumed a Lateral position on the carpet and gave myself up to Thought. After, I suppose, some nine minutes I sat up.

'We will be waiting for you at the cleaners tomorrow with a vehicle,' I said, emphasising each word. 'You will enter the vehicle, with your suit, and be driven to the church. On the way your suit will be neatly pressed -

WHILE IT IS ON YOU!'

His face was a study.

There were all too few hours left for preparation, for racing round to the builder's merchants, the camping equipment shop, the ironmongers, to say nothing of persuading Mr Marshall to lend us his Mobile Greengrocery van.

2.30 the next day saw my wife, son and I, in Mr Marshall's van, waiting outside the cleaners in Virginia Water. My wife had lit the two camping stoves and fixed the rubber tubing to the spouts of the two kettles. Jamie was keeping the engine running for a smooth getaway.

Nicholas emerged, clutching his clean but crumpled suit, and looking, I thought, a shade apprehensive.

Once Nick was in the van, Jamie let in the clutch and proceeded towards Sunninghill. Nick changed into his suit in a secluded corner by the cabbages and on my word of command assumed a prone position on the floor.

Rolling forward the two three-foot lengths of six-inch diameter, salt glaze pottery drainage pipes I deftly slipped them up Nick's legs. There was an awkward moment when his right shoe jammed in the pipe but a blow or two with the starting handle freed the foot and no time was lost. Polly's kettles were then on the boil and, on the word of command, she inserted the rubber tubes up the pipes.

We allowed the steam to play through the pipes for six minutes. I then slid the pipes away from the legs and Nick stood up for the next stage, which consisted of applying bulldog clips so as to form creases in the damp, hot fabric. Eighty of these were clipped on, twenty to each crease, back and front, both legs. As Nick sat on the tailboard of the van, dangling his legs in the airstream to dry off his trousers, we began on the jacket.

First we removed the jacket, replacing it with a heatproof waistcoat made by my wife from eighteen oven gloves sewn together. Next we dampened the jacket with water from the watering-can Mr Marshall used to freshen up his lettuces. We then replaced the jacket on Nick, and covered the entire surface of the jacket, sleeves as well, in ovenproof aluminium foil. After checking that Nick was completely foiled, I lit my little calor-gas blow torch and began playing it carefully over the foil, keeping it moving, watching for tell-tale puffs of steam which told me that the scheme was working.

At one point Nick seemed to slump.

'Are you all right?' I enquired, anxiously. 'Not the old ticker, vicar?'

But it was only some large potatoes which had fallen off a high rack, when Jamie had taken a right-hand bend at speed, and hit Nicholas on the head.

We stripped off the hot foil, held the jacket out of the window to cool it off, and the job was done.

At 2.49 precisely my son pulled up with a jerk outside the gates of Sunninghill church, a rain of assorted choice veg. descended upon us and Nick got out of the van and made his way towards the vestry door, looking smart and neat in his well-pressed suit.

He was still steaming a little here and there but we reckoned that anybody noticing it in church would assume it to be a kind of nimbus.

'Well,' said my wife, plucking a Brussels sprout from her hair. 'Thank goodness that's over.'

'Over?' I said, incredulity in my voice. 'Over? It hasn't really started yet. We are on our way to our first million with the Muir On-site Valet Van!'

'You don't really suppose you can make money with this . . . this . . .'

'Consider,' I said, my voice rising with boyish enthusiasm. 'It'll be the Fourth of June soon. Founder's Day at Eton. Statesmen, judges and millionaires trudging along Eton High Street, suits crumpled after sitting all day in deckchairs watching cricket. I step out of the van parked by the kerb. 'Touch up, my lord? Just step inside!' And then there's Henley Regatta. Hundreds of old chaps in little pink caps - Leanderthal Man - watching their sons skulling up and down and wondering how they are going to make the old blazer last through the week. 'Care for a spruce-up before your son wins the race, sir? Polly - put the kettles on!' Thank goodness that Nick started us going.'

'What are you trying to say?'

'Let us now press famous men, and the fathers at regattas!'

JOANNA LUMLEY

When I was nine, I had the most delicious party dress.
It was made of taffeta, dark
bronze in colour, with dark
green and red checks, and a
white broderie anglaise
collar. It had puffed sleeves
which were gathered in
above the elbow, and a
wide, hissy, slithery sash
around the waist. The skirt
was gathered, fairly full,
with a deep dark ruffle
round the hem. But best of
all was the petticoat:
buttercup yellow taffeta,
with the dark bronze taffeta
frill, two layers of it around
the bottom. I only wore it
twice as I was growing so
fast – it was given away. I've
never forgotten it.

THORA HIRD

I was sixteen and I was going to the Co-op Ball . . . in other words, 'The Lancaster and District Co-operative Society Annual Staff Ball', held at the Ashton Hall, Lancaster, 7.30 until 2 o'clock, tickets 5/- (or for readers who weren't born in 1927, twenty-five new pence!) including three-course dinner!

My best friend, Margaret, and I both worked at the Co-op. I was the cashier at Queen's Square Branch, Morecambe, and Margaret worked in the Office, so of course, snob value demanded we should attend. The trouble was, what to wear? The fashion was for handkerchief points on the skirt of *any* dress that pretended it *was* anything, so Doris Brown, 'the little woman round the corner', obliged. She was a smashing dressmaker.

The 'creation' was in eau-de-nil satin, with handkerchief points (of course) that were edged with eau-de-nil ninon. I wore pure silk stockings and brocade evening shoes with lavatory heels and a neat strap that fastened with a french paste button. My hair was put up in earphones (making me look just like I do as Ivy Unsworth in *In Loving Memory*). White gloves and a little brocade evening bag completed the ensemble, and there I was . . . what man could resist me? Oh, and I had my rimless glasses on as well!

Margaret and I caught a Ribble Bus to Lancaster (sixpence return – old money!) – we always travelled in style.

On arrival at The Ashton Hall we met many friends and eventually sat down to dinner. Oh, this was the life! The first course was mushroom soup and as the waiters started to serve, jollity and laughter filled the air.

I don't know how many of you know what a comedy trip is (well . . . for those of you who don't, I won't try and describe it – ask somebody – they'll do it for you), but that's what the waiter did as he was about to put my plate of soup in front of me! Whoops! My eau-de-nil satin lap was full of scalding hot mushroom soup that was seeping through onto my pure silk tights and burning my pure Lancashire thighs! Hecky plonk!! The entire gathering of Co-op employees heard my animal howl as I jumped in the air in agony. The

guests on my immediate left and right (slightly splashed with soup!) jumped up in sympathy wiping the dribbles of soup off their borrowed or hired dinner suits. As for the poor waiter, he stood transfixed, as though he was playing statues, his white serviette over his arm, his eyes glued on the soup-sodden apron of my dress.

Margaret (Peg to intimates) assisted me to the Ladies' Room, where I stood with mushroom soup dripping down my pure silk tights and tears dripping down my face. What to do? That was the question.

Although there is much to be said for the good old days, one thing that *cannot* be said is that there were dozens of handtowels and boxes of tissues in the Ladies! A spotlessly clean roller towel was hanging behind the door which, being at chest level, was no use when we'd washed the skirt of my satin dress and needed to dry it! Pathetically we tried to dry the soaking wet patch with our little lace-edged evening handkerchiefs, the result being, there I stood with a wet patch as big and round as a huge tray on the front of my eau-de-nil original model!

I caught sight of my face in the oval mirror over the wash basin. The tears had streaked my Potter and Moors Powder Cream Foundation and my bit of eye black was slightly adrift – watta sight. And then I started to laugh, and so did Peg. When we'd calmed down I did running repairs on my face and we went back to try and enjoy what was left of the dinner.

When the dancing started I was asked to dance by a very handsome Brylcremed young man. I answered him, 'I'm sorry but I cannot dance with a badly-stained dress!' to which he replied (sharp as a knife), 'I'm not a badly-stained dress' (oh, tee hee, watta comic!) 'and anyway, no one will see the stain when we're in a clinch!' Which was true, of course. I think I danced every dance for the rest of the evening – the wet patch dried as the heat of the Charleston whipped us all into an abandoned frenzy! By the time we were ready for the journey home on the bus it rather resembled a wrinkled prune.

The dress was ruined and there was nothing I could do about it, but that little eau-de-nil creation is tattooed on my memory, as is something else: we had *a wonderfully happy evening!!* That's the blessing of being young – you don't let anything unimportant worry you for long!

WENDY TOYE

Which of all the lovely costumes and dresses that I've been lucky enough to wear could be described as the most memorable? Could it be the beautiful evening frock that Motley designed for me to wear on the first night of my ballet, *Aucassin and Nicolette,* which I had choreographed for Dame Alicia Markova and Sir Anton Dolin's company? Motley had devised the 12th-century style sets and costumes like gossamer, and my dress matched them.

Or could it be the magnificent Infanta costume that Rex Whistler designed for me to wear in the ballet, *The Birthday of the Infanta?* He drew so carefully the makeup for me, too – I still have his signed sketch.

Or could it be the dress I wore in *The Golden Toy* at the Coliseum, with such a huge head-dress that at one performance I lost my balance and twirled myself over the footlights and into the orchestra pit, much to my embarrassment and the fury of the first violinist, on whom I landed? Or could it be . . .? Or could it be . . .?

And then it struck me – it had to be the little number I wore at The Great Charleston Ball at the Albert Hall in 1929. Sir Charles B. Cochran had dreamed up and organized this competition to decide who were the greatest Charleston dancers in Europe, and as I am sure you all know, Lew Grade won the Men's title. However, I am equally sure that you don't know that I won the Females'.

I was nine years old, and the only child entered. What a night – if I had been older I might have been petrified with nerves, but I was so young I didn't realize that I should have been nervous. (There is a great lesson in that.)

Among the judges were Fred Astaire, Ziegfeld, The Dolly Sisters, and many others. Hundreds of people were entered, and in my section the judges stood all round us and eliminated the unlucky ones in batches of about twenty each time. Our routines lasted about two minutes, and I guess I must

have done it at least thirty times, until I was in that great place dancing alone – the winner – Number 66.

My dress – my mother had made it, of course – was white and silver. It had a top of absolutely shapeless white velvet (for my absolutely shapeless figure), with a round neck and no sleeves, and the skirt was three frills of Brussels lace and tulle, with a spray of silver flowers hanging from the waist on the left side. I adored it. I had silver shoes with cut-outs at the side, low heels and buffskin soles to keep me from slipping on the ballroom floor.

And do you know, the only thing that worried me during the whole of that sophisticated, elegant evening, was: would my socks stay up?

MARJORIE PROOPS

Clothes accident prone – that's me. Inevitably when I put on something new or freshly cleaned after the last accident, I'll have another one.

Like upsetting the mayonnaise into the lap of my delicate floral frock at Henley when I did so want to look as elegant as all the posh guests – and in trying to mop up the damage, I splashed my host's impeccable blazer. He said he loved mayonnaise and I wasn't to worry about the spots, his wife would take care of it – so I wasn't too popular with her, either.

But my worst moment was at the customs counter when I was returning from a working trip to Brussels. I'd got married just a few weeks earlier and was wearing my trousseau undies beneath practical working gear. Neat skirts and shirts in those days. No nice easy jeans.

Anyhow, the customs man, delving into my suitcase said 'anything to declare' and just as I was about to murmur 'nothing' and try to look honest, I felt the waist elastic of my frilly silk and lace French knickers snap. And down slithered those knickers, round my ankles.

The customs man snorted with mirth, saying 'you've sure got plenty to declare' as I stepped out of my knicks, and as I bent to retrieve them, a nun, one of a party queuing up behind me, picked them up gingerly, face averted, as she handed them over.

Even now, decades later, I still shudder when someone says 'knickers'.

WENDY CRAIG

One of my most favourite-ever dresses was a cornflower blue chiffon number. A ball gown, it was a slim, column shape with a low-cut back and huge frills of taffetta for the sleeves. It was beautifully made, with weights around the hem and a pure silk lining, and it felt very expensive – which it was.

I am notorious for spilling things over my clothes when I'm out dining. I'm not sure whether this is caused by clumsiness or whether my co-ordination falls apart when faced with a stressful occasion. Anyway, this favourite of all dresses was bought for an awards presentation where I was to receive a scroll, as one of the most promising new-comers in a film.

It was as they say, a glittering evening, at one of London's famous hotels, and I felt terrific in this blue dress, with the added glamour of a false hair piece.

We sat down to dinner, and the first course was Sea Food Cocktail. As I gaily chatted and waved to friends around the room, a large spoonful of this fishy substance landed on my knee and slithered all the way down to my gold shoes. Horrified, I dabbed at it with my napkin, but to no avail. The South Sea Island dressing was absorbed into the chiffon as though it were on blotting paper. Reaching for the salt, I sprinkled the oily marks liberally and sat there pretending to laugh when people asked if I would like the pepper too.

My name was called, I rose to my feet, patted off the salt, and sidled up to the platform with my hands spread over the tell-tale marks. People must have thought I was in agony from shell-fish poisoning! Audrey Hepburn presented me with my scroll. Needless to say, she was without spot – in pristine white.

I could never get the marks out of that frock, but I keep it in a trunk, because in spite of everything I love it still.

BLOOMERS

BOB MONKHOUSE

I was about fourteen and it was in the *Beckenham Journal* and it made me laugh. The review described a variety show at the Penge Empire and said of the top-of-the-bill: 'Mr Max Wall exploded on stage.' Not much point in going to see him then, I thought. What a way to go.

At the time of writing Max is in his eighties, still working and as well as can be expected. As for me, I was twenty-one when I met and wrote comedy material for him and mentioned the review, 'They said you exploded on stage, Max.' 'Ah yes,' said the Great Man, 'it was something they put in the bread in those days. Show business is very hard on clothes.'

And so we dissolve to seven years later. I'm now twenty-eight and topping the bill myself in cabaret at the Savoy Hotel in London. By a wonderful stroke of luck the legendary Liberace has come into my life through the magic of ITV. His Sunday afternoon sessions of flamboyant piano-playing and winking have numbed the British with disbelief. It's a free gift for me that I bear a strong facial resemblance, so into my act he goes.

I had a black tail-suit made with Christmas tinsel fringed round the edges. The facing of the lapels was black gauze beneath which were hidden dozens of little torch bulbs. These were wired to heavy acid atteries in the tails. I wore a matching wig frosted with glitter and sat at a grand piano as the lighting came up slowly, revealing only my silhouette as I mimed the Liberace opening theme to a tape recording played through a speaker attached to the underneath of the Savoy's Steinway. The audience hooted and applauded.

When the pin-spot lit my head, the applause and the laughter became uncontrolled. I had to wait for it to subside before embarking on my parody of 'I'll Be Seeing You', Liberace's regular song. Some wicked satirical patter followed, the introduction of 'my mom' (played by a sexy little blonde actress called Carole Lesley who, I explained, was a walking miracle of cosmetic surgery), and the final song which ended with the tasteful climax of what was a pretty cruel lampoon - a stage blackout and the illumination of my jacket.

Boy, did I love that jacket! It was the biggest laugh I had ever got.

I had been playing to very good business and my booking had been extended by two weeks the night it happened. No one warned me because no one knew. The first I knew myself was during 'I'll Be Seeing You', when a section of the audience near the door broke into puzzling applause. A celebrity had entered the room but I couldn't make out who. As I continued with the act, the laughter took on an oddly excited note and a buzz of delighted chatter spread rapidly. It wasn't until the introduction of 'mom' and the spotlight following her wiggling walk around the perimeter of the stage that I saw him in a passing flash, sitting ringside. Yes, you're right. It was Liberace, in London on an unannounced visit.

I suppose I could have fled or died on the spot or changed my name or lost my mind or denied everything or blamed my parents or offered up my first-born. Instead, I finished the act as if in a trance.

Moments later I was slumped in the dressing-room as one transfixed by the enormity of his transgression, and wondering whether Liberace was powerful enough to have me feeding the fishes in the Thames before dawn, when Ethel Levy, the Savoy's booker, came in hurriedly.

'No time to change. Lee wants to see you at once.'

It was the walk to the scaffold. Still wearing my guilt, the sleazy tail-suit, I was shown into Liberace's suite. He was sitting at a grand piano with a small entourage around him. I stood there, unable to think of anything to say in mitigation for my insulting burlesque.

The Magnificent Showman rose, walked towards me with his arms extended, hugged me warmly and said, 'You were wonderful, Bob!' I think I said something quite witty like, 'Ar-hah-phnunph.'

'But come on, come over to the piano, let's open more champagne, and let's get to work on this!' he cried, waving everyone aside and leading me with his arm around the shoulders of my vulgar jacket. 'You must make the whole thing much more *evil*! Put in a big handbag, smothered in sequins! Camp it up! Look, I'll show you! I'll show you how to do Liberace so well you'll make me *hate* you!' And for the next hour and a half, he showed me and I learned.

My Liberace impression became standard fare for me on TV and a must for my summer seasons. My jacket was rewired and mended and hand-cleaned again and again. I could have had a new one made but this was the magic garment to me now, the one that Lee himself had embraced. I tell you again, I loved that jacket. I suppose a love affair like that isn't meant to last.

Nothing had gone right with the preparation of the show. There were arguments about the script, disagreement over music, and I was sorry I'd taken the booking. Most comedians are wary of playing the Albert Hall anyway. It's too big for the use of any but the broadest grimaces and gestures and in 1962 the sound system was unsuitable for fast patter. But it was the right venue for the occasion. We were launching a new car to the motor trade and they had booked me to host the first part, then change into Liberace and drive the new car on to the stage. The car was to be edged in light bulbs but the electrical problems were a nightmare. So was the last minute decision to turn me into a Christmas tree.

'Your jacket won't stand out next to the car when we black out and switch the bulbs on,' they told me. 'We'll have to fit you up with equally bright bulbs. You're not to worry, we know what we're doing.'

I looked like Blackpool Tower in October, light bulbs sprouting all over me and two long black cables snaking out of my trousers at each ankle. All possibility of comic effect was gone. I was a serious safety hazard. But I was not to worry, they knew what they were doing.

That night the presentation was going smoothly enough, the audience seemed pleased, and I finished my first-half duties feeling vaguely confident. Even as I was strapped and plugged and bound into my now unrecognizable tail-suit, I thought everything might be all right. I climbed awkwardly into the small car, heard my announcement and the Liberace theme, drove up the ramp on to the stage, climbed out as best I could and stood beside the motor, waving my arm. On cue, the Albert Hall darkened and the bulbs came on.

The car was okay.

I did what Max Wall was said to have done at the Penge Empire.

I exploded on stage.

Those who were there that night still speak of it. They saw the car's outline in brightly shining bulbs for just a moment. Then its brilliance was eclipsed as its driver blew up. My tiny dark outline flickered into a white-hot starburst. A plume of heat and steam and fizzing electrical fire streamed up from my shoes to my scorching wig. I must have looked like Joan of Arc in formal wear.

Afterwards, as two St John Ambulance men applied ointments to my singed bits hand kept repeating, 'You were really very lucky, you know' and 'What on earth made you do it?', I saw my Liberace jacket for the last time. It was burned and torn, its skeleton of cables and wires exposed, its hundred sockets fused and choked, its tinsel hanging forlornly. A cleaner was stuffing it into a bin. It's
like the blessed Max Wall
said.

Show business is very hard on clothes.

Bob Monkhouse and Liberace in Liberace's Suite at The Savoy, 1956.

JOHN JUNKIN

Due to an aversion to aeroplanes and a belief that, if the Lord had meant us to fly, we would have all been born nearer Gatwick, I turned to cruise ships for a holiday in 1970, and my first one was a real culture shock. It was on a ship called the *Andes* and I still believe that no one had told the owners about World War II, because it was sheer, unadulterated, pre-war luxury.

Included in the tickets was a brochure, with instructions - not requests - about the proper wear on board ship, including the phrase 'evening dress will be worn at dinner.' Now, as one brought up in the East End, and having spent much of the previous ten years like most actors - surviving in bed-sits - my need for a dress suit had been minimal, but I decided 'when in Rome' and duly purchased one.

The cruise was one of those rare occasions in life when reality lived up to the brochure and I spent the first four days in a wonderful fantasy world. There was one steward for every four passengers and each evening when I returned to my cabin to dress for dinner, there, neatly laid out, was everything that I required. The suit was pressed, the shoes cleaned, even the cuff links were placed ready in the double cuffs: and, at some time, prior to the dinner gong, there would be a discreet knock at the door, and my steward, Stephen, would enquire if there was anything I required. I was beginning to feel like Bertie Wooster, until the fourth evening, when I returned to the cabin as Stephen was completing his tasks. He turned as I came in.

'White dinner jacket tomorrow, Mr Junkin,' he said. 'We'll be in the Mediterranean.'

This was a piece of information that had slipped through my net. I was severely taken aback.

'I ...er ...I ... don't *have* a white dinner jacket,' I mumbled. There was an infinitesimal pause. Stephen's sigh was inaudible, his expression barely changed by a whisker, but I knew I had let him down.

'Very well, Mr Junkin,' he murmured, '*Black* dinner jacket tomorrow, then.' And he left the cabin.

Dinner that night tasted like ashes, the wine was sour, the company boring. Through my mind ran a newsreel of the scorn with which Stephen was being greeted below the decks as he confessed to my failing.

'No white DJ, Stephen' I heard them sneering, 'dear, oh dear, you've got a right yob there.'

By midnight, if I could have found a convenient life raft, I would have cast myself adrift. Instead I went to bed, but, be warned: uneasy lies the head that doesn't own a white DJ.

By morning, I could stand it no longer, and I was waiting outside the ship's shop when it opened.

Did they stock white dinner jackets?

They did.

Did they have one my size?

They did. Just the one.

In a frenzy, in case some other ignoramus with the same chest size should come in and pluck it from my grasp, I paid for it and returned to the cabin.

When Stephen came in for his nightly ritual it was hanging *outside* the wardrobe, and when I came down to dress, it was neatly laid out with the rest of my evening wear. Nothing, naturally, was said, but I knew that I had saved both our faces in the nick of time.

I wore the white dinner jacket each evening for the next two weeks, always immaculately sponged and pressed and, by the end of that time, I was no longer Bertie Wooster. I was Simon Templar.

When we left the Med on the return trip I was sad to see it packed away, and felt my glamour quotient was severely reduced by returning to the old black jacket.

After the cruise it was consigned to my wardrobe from whence it probably made two excursions in the next ten years, but it was money well spent.

I never saw Stephen again, but if he should read this, it's still in the wardrobe - and thanks.

LES DAWSON

The first time I wore my pantomime dame knickers, the elastic broke quite audibly and they drooped to such an extent, my posterior in all its pristine glory lay revealed for all mankind to see.

A hooligan in the stalls made a remark on the lines of 'Cor blimey, the moon's full tonight.'

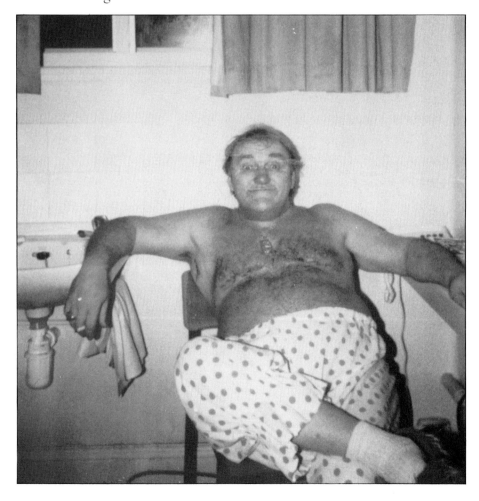

SUSANNAH YORK

'Come as you would for a hot summer's evening in the South of France' said the invitation to 'The Greengage Summer's' première. My yellow shorts? Thong sandals? Surely they wouldn't mean a bikini . . . ? I opted for safety, bought some cotton in the market and Mrs Hyde, my landlady, made me a floral mini dress for £2. Off on the back of the scooter to the Odeon, Leicester Square, proud at having so perfectly balanced my responsibilities as 'the star', with the demands of summer gaiety. Tears of rage and humiliation were to follow as producers and distributors bullied, pleaded and harangued me to race back home and come back like 'a star'.

'In a *limousine*, Susannah, and a glamorous evening gown.'

'But the invitaion *said*. . .'

I didn't of course: and still agonise over the 'dress code' on a formal invitation.

MARCIA FALKENDER

This is the story of a party dress, a net and chiffon confection, I wore as a child. Unfortunately, just before the party, my brother had discovered on the hall floor, what he took to be little bars of chocolate. The were in fact ex-Lax samples put through doors as an advertising gimmick. He gave them all to me and I ate them up happily. I went to that party in the pretty net and chiffon dress, but wearing three or four pairs of thick knickers underneath which were very uncomfortable and embarrasing. I have remembered that dress and that party all my life.

In my adult life, it's not an outfit I remember, but a pair of shoes.

It was the Sixties. I had received this surprise gift from a friend: a pair of seemingly beautiful and very glamorous evening slippers. They really were beautiful. They were also transparent - they looked like glass slippers - with white satin bows on the front.

I wore them, with a long white satin caftan embroidered in gold, for an official dinner and reception at No.10 Downing Street. I felt so proud and was so thrilled with the shoes.

But, alas, it was a very warm summer evening. As I talked and chatted, imagine my horror when I looked down at my feet to admire the shoes, only to find they had completely steamed up! No longer transparent, no longer glamorous, and quite obviously steamed up, I took the first opportunity to slip away to cool them off, and myself and to recover from the embarrassment.

Early days, with my brother, in front, and, far right, No 10 days.

TOYAH WILLCOX

The story I would like to relate concerns a dress I first saw in the *Observer* Magazine. It was a glossy photo that caught my eye, of a woman crying in a churchyard. She was wearing a very tight, shiny, rubber dress – probably the most stunning dress I have ever seen, because of its simplicity. It started under the arms and ended above the knee, and it was skin tight.

The next day I found the designer in a small, undiscovered shop and bought this magical dress.

Off the body it looked small and deflated and I wondered if I'd done the right thing. I had a photo session that day and when I held the dress up to the photographer, Terance Donovan, he laughed.

I sulked off to the dressing-room to dress. After half an hour, a bottle of talcum powder and a tin of Mr Sheen, I emerged, and the dress 'did us proud'. Mind you, it took two dressers to zip it up, and when on, it had to be polished.

This dress became famous. It was 1985 and I wore it all over the continent, until one day I was filming a song in a German film studio.

The set looked like a fall-out shelter, the camera work was immaculate (in Germany it usually is). By the time we'd rehearsed and got the lighting correct, my dress had caused a sensation. The studio became full of onlookers, many of them tourists who'd come to see the set of *Boat,* a famous German series. So I'd say, in all, about a hundred or so people had collected in this vast studio to look at my dress apart from hear me sing.

It was a very hot day, I'd run through my number seven times and I was breaking out in a sweat. The lights were powerful and hot.

We went for a take – all was well. Then, just before the end, my nice rubber dress became even 'more' famous and stole the show. It slid right off – leaving me to rapturous applause.

JULIE BURCHILL

In 1976, when I was a little punk of sixteen, I had a beautiful pair of leather bondage trousers. I don't know if you've ever seen a pair, but bondage trousers were what punks wore, and they were so called because they had a strap connecting the knees. You could walk in them, but it was a struggle. To further complicate matters, these trousers were *tight*.

One day I was crossing a very busy road in West London with a gang of comrade punks. It was such a busy road that crossing it was not encouraged and a pedestrian flyover was provided. To dissuade people from crossing, a long fence ran down the island in the middle. Of course, being punks and of a profoundly disobedient disposition, we ignored the flyover. We legged it to the island in the middle of the road, and vaulted over. At least, the others did.

I stuck. My bondage strap caught in the metal and I just sat there looking surprised. The trousers themselves were much too tight to make reaching down and disentangling the strap a possibility. So I just sat there.

My friends thought this was tremendously funny. So funny that they went off and left me. I don't know if you can imagine how humiliating it is to have to perch on a metal fence in the middle of an extremely busy thoroughfare for three quarters of an hour while drivers scream with laughter and slow down to take a closer look until a policeman comes along and unties you, but I would very much advise against trying it.

JOANNA DAVID

In 1983 I was playing Varya in *The Cherry Orchard* at the Yvonne Arnaud Theatre.

In one particular scene I had to put a cloth on a table and then walk upstage and talk about going on a pilgrimage.

I heard the audience giggling and whispering and couldn't think what had happened. To my horror I realized I'd dragged the table-cloth away with me – it was attached to a very important part of my costume – *Varya's keys!*

I attempted to look calm and replaced the cloth, but inwardly I was shaking.

THELMA BARLOW

I think I have known from being a very little girl that I was merely a figure of fun in the scheme of things, but at one time in my life, in an effort to be taken seriously I added to the list of actress, wife, and mother – the role of craftswoman and hobbyist.

The hobbies knew no bounds, and amongst them one winter was the gentle skill of crochet.

Now every December 9th we celebrate yet another birthday of 'Coronation Street' - this year it reaches the remarkable figure of 28 - but for the 16th birthday party I had crocheted a full-length turquoise dress. In the doubtful assumption that I work better under pressure this was only ready and pressed on the night before the event and the last button stitched on during a lull in the recording in the studio that day of the party.

Triumphantly I tried the dress on again - HORROR! Suddenly it was six inches too short! The reason, of course, was that the damp pressing had stretched the yarn and now it had sprung back to it's proper length. With one hour to go I started to crochet around and around the wretched skirt at breakneck speed ... almost finished - good! The call came to leave the dressing room and go into the studio and record the last two scenes of the day. I laid the dress down, grabbed Miss Riley's handbag, hurried along two corridors and was just about to enter the studio when a colleague called to me 'What on earth are you trailing along behind you?' 'Woe is me, for I am undone' would have been an apt reply, for the yarn from my dress had unravelled the newly crocheted hem, caught as it was in the clasp of the handbag, and, like the trail of a snail through a line of lettuce it followed my progress through the long corridors of Granada Television.

I think that evening I tried to give the impression that ankle-length dresses were extremely fashionable again, but I gave the dress away soon afterwards to a taller friend who liked her calves well-covered!

ANGIE RICHARDS

Some weeks ago, my best friend Tina Martin went into hospital for a major op. Her husband, kids and all her friends rallied round with love and support and presents. I thought – 'I know, I'll knit her something – that will be so personal.' So I purchased the wool, the needles and the pattern and proceeded with enthusiasm. My jumper grew very fast and I did have a little trouble with the front, back, sleeves, armholes and neck.

However, soon it was finished and I gave it to Tina – who immediately put it on and expressed her delight and said she loved it – especially as I had knitted it with my own hands. We both agreed we *liked* large sweaters – so roomy and comfortable. She told me later that after the operation, one day, she put the sweater on and told the ward sister, 'My best friend knitted this for me.' Sister replied, 'I trust she was not too offended when you severed the relationship.'

Tina says my sweater is still growing and her kids love it – every time they see their mum in it there is laughter all over the house. She is now completely recovered and we both believe that because she laughed so much over my sweater, her recovery was that much faster!

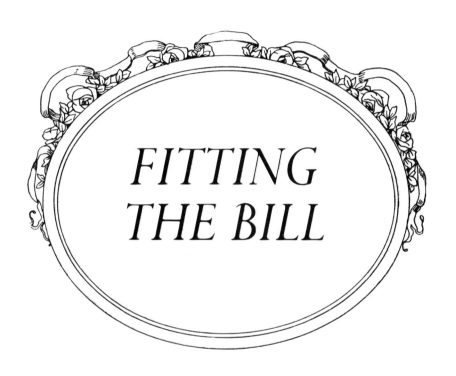

FITTING
THE BILL

STANLEY BAXTER

When I decided a couple of years ago to do a political spoof using the *Wizard of Oz* characters – Dorothy, the Scarecrow, the Tin Man and the Cowardly Lion – in my annual TV special. I almost at once began to envisage how uncomfortable the Tin Man was going to be. Then I got to thinking about the metallic make up. How difficult, I wondered, would it be to remove?

In the event the Cowardly Lion turned out to be the most uncomfortable costume I've *ever* worn, and the Tin Man the most comfortable – it was as light as a feather, and good old Max Factor does a silver that comes off more easily than their negro colours.

When I first approached the lady who was making the costumes I said, 'Now, regarding the materials for the Tin Man – unlike him – have a heart.' She certainly did. It was a masterpiece.

MARGARET THATCHER

As a working lady, I choose clothes which are plain but have a good cut. Like others in business, politics or executive position, clothes are really a background to the personality. My dark navy silk dress has brought me good luck. I like this one very much. I had it made in 1982. I wore it in the Falklands year, to New York to address a full assembly of the United Nations and it came through that all right. So, as I say, when I do not know quite what to wear, this is the old faithful and it will do me well. It is just good, plain and classic.

MARTIN JARVIS

'Borrow a bra from yer mother or yer girlfriend, Martin, stuff it with yer football socks and Bob's yer Auntie . . .'

Not, in fact, an early incitement to transvestism, merely my English teacher advising me on how to prepare for my role as Lady Capulet in our school production of *Romeo and Juliet*. Having no girlfriend despite normal adolescent wish-fulfilment, and not being on bra-borrowing terms with my mother, I opted for just the socks. I cut an odd figure on our first night. Curiously contoured – and strangely unbalanced, too, in all other aspects of Mama Capulet: the haughty strut, the breaking voice, gash of red at the mouth and the black plimsolls peeking from beneath my Renaissance frock. I was a riot; and possibly the only Lady C in recent memory to enjoy the kind of comedy success normally reserved for a Widow Twankey or an Ugly Sister. It was of course the Costume that did it.

Thinking over some of the 'costumes I have known', it was brought home to me how much an actor's well-being depends on a comfortable relationship with his or her outfit. If the cap doesn't fit better not wear it.

I remember having a fitting (if not a fit) for my part as the smooth anti-hero in *The Heiress*. I dared to mention to Desmond, the toupéed wardrobe master, that the costume wasn't right. It had a crutch that would have accommodated an elephant. Desmond was appalled. 'Don't know what you're worrying about, duckie,' he said. 'Tony Britton wore this cozzie – he was very pleased with it.' I couldn't think of an appropriate reply, though my admiration for Tony Britton – actor and man – thereafter knew no bounds.

I encountered no such problems in my first professional engagement. Indeed, as the Ghost of Christmas Future in a Theatre-in-the-Round musical version of *A Christmas Carol,* I was delighted with my voluminous black robes and monkish cowl. Mine was a non-speaking, non-singing role, but rewarding nevertheless, as my job was to stand centre-stage and point to the Future a good deal. I sometimes had to guess where the Future was as I couldn't actually see anything – concealed within my vast hood. The climax came as

Scrooge grasped me in terror, shook me, and I crumpled to the floor, an apparently empty mound of Nathan's best worsted. Then, in the ensuing black-out and still enveloped in my ghostly robes, I had to grope my way as best I could from the stage. One night, however, intoxicated by the unexpected applause, I lost all sense of direction and found myself, like Blind Pugh, tapping people's arms and legs as I felt my way towards the exit. Unhappily they were not the limbs of my fellow actors. Oh God! I was among the audience. What should I do? The lights would be up again in a moment. Nothing for it but to make for the double doors at the back of the auditorium. I groped forward in the darkness, ignoring the puzzled exclamations of entranced theatre-lovers who had felt something quick and strange touch them up as it went by.

At last I stumbled through the doors but, struggling out of my robes and blinking at the unaccustomed brightness, I saw to my horror that I was even more off course than I had thought. I was in the street at the side of the theatre and was excellently lit by beams from a convenient lamp-post. I had crashed through the fire exit and was now in full view of half the stalls and some very curious passers-by. As I stood there, shivering, a large portion of the appreciative audience were intrigued to discover, as they gazed out into the night, that the Ghost of Christmas Future sported only a jock-strap beneath his monkish garb. I'm probably the only Dickensian ghost who has had to knock on the stage door with his costume under his arm and ask to be let in.

Luckily, my failure in this mute role did not reach the ears of Sir Bernard Miles, who generously gave me five lines as the effete Prince Cosmo in his production of *Galileo* at the Mermaid Theatre. He warned me to take care of my beautiful white satin uniform. 'That lovely costume cost two hundred and fifty pounds, Martin,' he told me. 'Pieces of eight, pieces of eight.' (A parrot was defecating on his shoulder at the time.) I was only earning eighteen pounds a week, so my outfit was far more important than I was. I minced gingerly for the entire run.

Surely, I imagined, nothing untoward, sartorially speaking, could happen in television. And when Verity Lambert offered me my first major role as

Prince Helio in *Dr Who,* I was thrilled. The big break. Six episodes as the monarch of my very own planet. Many scenes with William Hartnell.

'Have you seen the costume designs yet, Martin?' asked my attractive employer, handing me several large sheets of paper. 'Oh, thanks, Verity,' I replied suavely, secretly wondering if she'd like a drink in the BBC Club afterwards. I glanced down at the drawings. . . . Oh no. I was – a butterfly. A giant butterfly. Furry black and white striped body. Black legs. Black and white face, black skull cap and black, bulbous eyes. Long black antennae. And, oh dear, wings. 'Fancy a drink, Martin . . .?'

I don't think I shall ever forget my time as Prince of the Butterflies. The embarrassed glances of other actors in the canteen, smugly normal in their Z-cars raincoats. The problem of trying not to get my wings caught in the lift doors. And the Kirby's Flying Ballet harness biting into my crutch as I swung uneasily from rock to rock, calling out in a high-pitched tenor, 'Ah, Doctor – welcome to my planet. . . .'

At least there'll be no costume problems on radio, I thought, as I sauntered along to Broadcasting House one morning to begin recording my part as Prince Andrei in *War and Peace.* A bit of a surprise, therefore, when I was handed an ancient pair of heavy-duty BBC 'Sound Effects Shoes' which I was to wear at the Battle of Borodino. Were they really necessary? Oh yes, I was assured, they had been worn in the past by Richardson, Redgrave and Gielgud, and were vital to the audio picture. They were certainly unique: large, with laces, and painted bright blue, with yellow numbers on the toe caps – for security reasons, apparently. Security? I joked. Did they think Sir John might have taken a fancy to them and sneaked off down Regent Street after a recording, still wearing them? The unsmiling reaction seemed to suggest that you can't be too careful. No problem, though. I climbed into them and paraded my troops. Dostoevsky meets Minnie Mouse.

It wasn't until that night as I was leaving the building that I felt a heavy hand on my shoulder. 'Just a minute, sir.' I turned to find myself staring up into the eyes of a large Commissionaire. He looked down. I followed his gaze. My Russian triumph had, after all, gone to my head and I had forgotten my feet. There, on the end of my battle-weary legs, still rested the effective electric-blue footwear with the racy yellow toes, lending an unexpectedly psychedelic glow to the hallowed portals of Broadcasting House. I looked upwards again at this stern guardian of BBC security. 'Oh, thanks,' I said. 'You can't be too careful.'

Actors, not surprisingly, don't really feel secure without the right clothes. Whilst rehearsing Alan Ayckbourn's *Woman in Mind* it took me some time to inhabit the smug world of the Reverend Gerald Gannett and his sad wife Susan, played by Julia McKenzie. I was pleased with my brand new, open-toed sandals, happy with my half-mast grey flannel trousers, and thrilled with my clerical shirt and collar. I wore them at rehearsals daily. But I couldn't find the right cardigan. How could I ever hope to be the vicar without the perfect cardy?

Then one morning as we broke for coffee, Julia said, 'Martin, there are cardigans at the Oxfam shop near the Old Vic.' I raced away at once, taking the opportunity as I ran to 'scuff up' my sandals in the gutter to wear them in. Ignoring the curious glances of passers-by who wondered what this ecclesiastic figure was up to, I sped to the Oxfam shop and asked to see their cardigans. From the bottom of a pile a wonderous, baggy, plum-coloured garment was produced. I tried it on. 'Bless you,' I cried. And I knew finally that I was the real Reverend Gannett when the Irish lady behind the counter took my five pound note, smiled at me and said, 'There now, that'll be warm on your back, Father!'

In Shakespeare it's tights, in Restoration comedy it's breeches and cravats, and in the new British movie *Buster* it was, for me, raincoats. As Inspector Jack Mitchell of the Yard I wanted a raincoat of style and élan, circa 1963 – in other words, a Gannex. Sadly there was no Gannex to be bought or hired – not even for ready money. The days of Harold Wilson's sartorial example are long gone, but one day, staring gloomily at my research pictures, I remembered it was Joseph Kagan who had manufactured those splendid garments. Soon I was on the phone to Gannex Mills in Yorkshire and Mr Michael Kagan was delighted to help. 'We don't make them any more, but for you – we'll make one!' Director and crew breathed easy again – Jarvis had got his Gannex, shooting could continue. Only trouble was, it made a curious rubbery noise as I moved which drove the sound man mad. So the only custom-built 1988 Gannex in the land makes but a fleeting appearance in the film. If you spot a noisy, billowing, waterproof tent moving slowly like Birnam Wood towards the errant train robber – that's my raincoat.

I'm sure it'll come in useful in the winter, anyway. But perhaps the most genuinely useful accoutrement I have ever worn in the pursuance of my professional duties was my Nazi helmet. Dressed as a German officer, I was strapped by a willing team into a parachute harness and hoisted on a crane high, high into the Bavarian sky until the whole of Munich, it seemed, was spread out and spinning crazily below me. I was thinking how much happier I had been as a Dr Who butterfly when I heard a voice floating up from below. I looked down. I could just make out the tiny figure of our manic American director as he raised his megaphone and bawled up at me, 'Martin – in this shot try to look scared . . .!' It was lucky I had my helmet up there with me. Useful? Oh yes, I was sick in it.

LULU

I really enjoy getting into costume for a part, but Peter Pan is probably my favourite. With hardly any makeup, cropped hair and boobs completely flattened – what could be simpler!

RUSS ABBOT

Statistics on the Fat
Man Suit: 7 ½ metres
of cloth, chest and
waist 87 inches
Trouser zip – 26
inches – from an
anorak. Largest suit
made in the West End.

GORDEN KAYE

Predictably, I fear, my favourite garment cannot be anything other than the apron that I just donned in September 1982 to cover the (ever increasing) mid portions of René Antois, the hapless Café proprietor in *'Allo 'Allo!*

Approximately 5 years, 28 TV episodes, and 475 stage performances later, I still find the character incomplete without my wrap-around protector. Given its location and the subject uppermost in René's mind, my fondness for the apron would give any psychoanalyst a field-day!

ERNIE WISE

When I was a kid in show business, about ten years old, I wore some strange comedy outfits – some of Leeds and Bradford's ideas of comedy. I wore a little bowler hat, a cut-down evening dress suit (a safety-pin holding the jacket), a black shoe lace for a tie, and little red clogs.

I also had various outfits made from large check curtain material. Mind you, I didn't feel a fool. I thought it was quite normal.

UNDRESS

ALAN BENNETT

The one outfit that has consistently embarrassed me in the clothes department has been my birthday suit. The (relatively few) other people who have seen it confirm this view.

DUDLEY MOORE

I remember once, when I was a young boy, I had a beautiful long-panted wedding suit made for me of satin and I was going to be a 'page of honour' or whatever one called it in England. However, I have a feeling that I never got to wear it except for a photo taken at the time, which I can't seem to find anymore. The only other strange bit of clothing that I ever wore was a purple suit made out of velvet that I had made by a tailor in London. I never did get to wear it! I think I had it made because it was 'strangely outrageous'!

During the course of various sketches I've done over the years, I have however worn clothes to make me look a little bit like a combination of my mother and Dame Myra Hess. I've dressed up in a long gown with huge lifts underneath, so that I would become taller than my erstwhile comic partner Peter Cook, who at 6'2" generally towered over me. I wore the traditional Roman gear when I was Eno Barbus in a college production of Antony and Cleopatra. I think my favourite garb nowadays is to be in a robe and socks and generally 'slob' around the house!

RONNIE CORBETT

In the swimsuit that his mother knitted for him. His comment: 'What a funny place to hide your holiday money!'

TERRY WOGAN

The outfit I remember best was a simple loincloth, of rough hempen weave, which I wore when I was an Assyrian slave. No, I'm not doing a Shirley MacLaine, it wasn't in a previous existence, but on the stage of the Gaiety Theatre Dublin, during a grand opera season.

The opera was *Aida*, and the scene was the Grand March. The loincloth I had agreed to wear after a deal of haggling, but I had refused point-blank to cover myself from head to toe in revolting cocoa-butter, which according to the Producer, was what the smart Assyrian slave was wearing that year. So what the paying customers saw was the palest slave ever to come shambling out of Assyria. No wonder they handed the lead tenor the fruit . . .

"Like Miss Rigg, I just felt it was right for this particular play"

"Psst, young fellah!—Just one step closer to our little Diana and I'll blow your head off!"

KEITH MICHELL

It was probably the first stage costume I ever wore. We did a concert in the local hall at the country town where I grew up. The hall was used for Saturday night dances and Sunday church and then any other concerts they had such as school concerts. I had to sing a song with a girl called Una, who I was mad about at the age of six, and the song was called 'Where are you going to, my Pretty Maid' - you may even know it? - and she wore a pink satin dress and bonnet and little black patent shoes and white socks and I had a pale blue satin jacket and black knee breeches and silver cardboard buckles on my shoes and I think I even had some sort of top hat. It probably looked ghastly but I thought the whole thing was a creative masterpiece and got my first sensation of the magical transformation of stage costumes, a sensation which I still have every time I do a new show!

Alternatively, I think I shall always remember appearing starkers on stage with Diana Rigg. In fact we were the first two straight actors in London to wear nothing at all on stage. We were of course extremely nervous about it which is why there are no photographs but I remember it fondly - of course! - particularly one night when Di sent a message across to me before the entrance that she wouldn't be appearing completely naked this evening: she had a sticking plaster on her toe. On the opening night in Brighton it was very low key dramatic lighting and in Birmingham on the opening night, in the middle of the scene, the lights went up to full. 'I saw you pick up your jewels' said Di 'and Tom and Jerry off'.

RICHARD HARRIS

———————— • ————————

When I was fifteen I stood five feet one, weighed six stone eight and girls kicked sand in my face. All of which changed when I discovered Charles Atlas and Dynamic Tension. Or rather, when Scully discovered it. He came up to me one day at school, grabbed me by the throat and said 'Don't mess me about, how would you like to improve your body for a mere ten bob, one nod for yes, two nods for I'm not interested and don't you bloody dare'. So I gave him the nod and he put me down and explained that he and his best mate Meredith had seen this Charles Atlas body-building advert and wanted to send off for the course but as it cost five quid, which was four quid above their budget, they were enlisting volunteers to make up the difference and build our bodies accordingly.

There were ten of us in all – which worked out rather well because, when the course came back, it consisted of ten roneoed pages, each with a title like 'How To Develop Arms of Steel' or 'Legs Of Iron' or 'The Chest Of Hercules' – the idea being that each of us would take a page and develop that part of his anatomy for a month and then swop pages and move on to another bit. All of which sounds very fair if you don't happen to be five feet one and six stone eight and the runt of the pack. When the pages were handed out by Messrs Scully and Meredith, I got 'How To Develop And Control Your Bladder'. So while everyone else was developing these massive arms and chests and thighs, I was concentrating on stemming the flow of urine. Quite what the object of the exercise was, I never really understood, but the idea was that you started to have a pee, stopped, held it for a count of ten seconds, resumed peeing for a count of ten, stopped, held it for ten, then resumed. Next time, you held it for fifteen seconds. Next time, twenty. And so on. Come the end of the month I was holding it for an hour and a half and no-one wanted to swap pages with me. For the next year, I spent more time in the school lavatory than I did in bed. You see, body-building is addictive. You go through the pain barrier and you get hooked. And I admit it, I was hooked.

Kids used to back away when they came into the lav and found me staring at the porcelain mumbling twenty three thousand nine hundred and twenty four, twenty three thousand nine hundred and twenty five...rumours went round and a member of the sixth form threatened to beat me up if I tried anything funny.

Maybe because of the peculiar way I was starting to walk, Scully and Meredith took pity on me and let me share their pages. We became obsessed. All we ever thought about was the body beautiful. The male body beautiful. Girls? What's girls? We joined a bodybuildng club, spent five nights a week pumping iron and our bodies developed accordingly. Weekends we used to lie around by the Serpentine in an attempt to bronze our huge frames.Sun lotion was in short supply in those days so we used either Brylcreem or cooking fat. Sounds terrible, smelled terrible, but it's true. We shaved our legs and smothered ourselves in grease and had photographs taken by a man named Basil in the hope of getting them published in *Health And Strength* magazine. Our hero was an American named Steve Reeves who had a forty eight inch chest and a twenty four inch waist and who ended up playing Hercules in Italian movies. And all the time we were pushing onwards and outwards. Meredith got into the final of the Mister Universe Under Five Foot Six Competition, I won a Ninety Day Self-Improvement Competition sponsored by H and S magazine and had my photo published. Scully developed an eighteen inch neck and, to test its strength, we used to hang him in his fathers shed. He stood on a stool with a noose around his neck and, on a given signal, we took the stool away and he dangled. It was his idea, by the way. When his face reached a particular shade of blue-black we replaced the stool. His record was twenty seven seconds and, being the perfectionist, he used to get really angry if we panicked and replaced the stool before his face had reached the exact-right colour. As he said, what's the point if you don't do things proper?

Most Saturday nights we'd go out as a threesome, dressed identically . . . Tony Curtis haircut, white tee-shirt proclaiming in blue print that we were members of The National Amateur Bodybuilders' Association, pegged trousers, yellow socks, ox-blood brothel creepers with plaited tops and crepe soles. We never kept our arms by our sides but arranged them as though we were carrying two large but invisible rolls of carpet. How else to advertise the size of our latisimmus dorsi?

Scully's family moved up north suddenly and we didn't keep in touch, so what became of him and his eighteen inch neck I've no idea. I lost contact with Meredith when we went different ways doing National Service. I did bump into him once about ten years ago: he was very fat and it was impossible to believe that this was once that. All my muscles disappeared and up to about a year ago when I stopped smoking, I was as thin as a lath. I once told my children stories of my iron-pumping days and they clearly didn't believe a word. Looking at me now, who can blame them? Right, I thought; I'll show you. I knew I had one of my photographs somewhere and sorted it out. Me in my posing brief, legs shaven, covered in cooking oil. On second thoughts, perhaps not. I've got enough trouble. I tried to find one of me in my walking-out uniform, but there weren't any. Which was a pity. I think they might have been quite impressed by the Tony Curtis and the brothel creepers with the plaited tops and crepe soles.

SHERIDAN MORLEY

I am not, I fear, widely known for my sense of costume: as a friend once noted, 'Sheridan only ever gets dressed in order not to appear naked'

FOLLIES

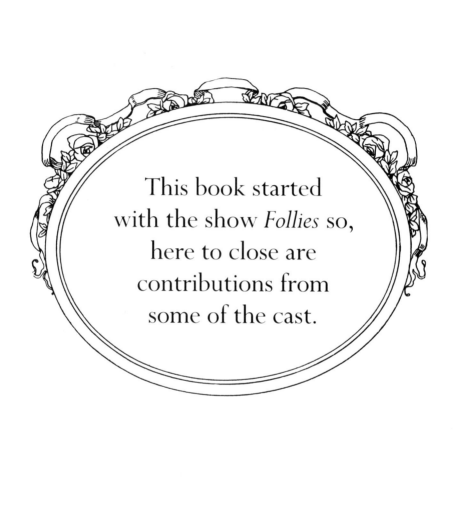

This book started
with the show *Follies* so,
here to close are
contributions from
some of the cast.

DIANA RIGG

The hated garment was a camel 'shopping' coat of my mother's, dyed navy blue and recycled as my school coat. I was thirteen, had just developed a waist, and everything had to be tightly belted to proclaim this phenomenon. The coat was square, and bulky, and nothing short of a fan-belt would draw it in. I cried, pleaded and threatened suicide, but my parents were resolute, so to school in it I went. Every morning I had to pass a crowd of schoolboys at a bus stop, and I remember sucking both cheeks in as I did so, trying to give them a hint of the slender, sinuous body beneath the navy blue mound. They must have thought I was potty.

PEARL & TEDDY JOHNSON

Early in 1961 we were appearing regularly on the Arthur Haynes series of weekly television shows. For one of our vocal spots we put together a medley of Old Tyme Cockney Music Hall songs. We performed them around an old costermonger's barrow that was located in a typical London street scene. To add a final touch of colour and authenticity, we were dressed in Pearlie King and Queen costumes.

We had such a tremendously favourable reaction from friends and viewers that we thought it would be a pity if the whole presentation was disposed of after just a three minute TV exposure. If it was any good, why not include something like it in out stage act?

We made some enquiries as to the cost of manufacture of two Pearlie costumes and got the surprise of our lives. Pearl buttons, we were told, were very rare and very expensive. If you did manage to find the hundreds that were needed for two costumes, they were then very expensive to tailor. Each one had to be individually sewn on, by hand. It was going to cost as much as £600 to have Pearlie King and Queen costumes on our backs. This was in 1961 and today's equivalent would probably be in the region of £6,000.

O.K. We were prepared to pay £600 but ... suppose the Cockney medley proved a flop? Suppose audiences gave us the thumbs down for it? All that money would have been wasted.

We once purchased an American Civil War uniform for Teddy to wear while he sang 'The Yellow Rose of Texas'. Before he could wear it on stage the song had faded in popularity. Would two pearl-buttoned costumes worth £600 now rest in peace alongside our US Army surplus, in a bashed up old suitcase in the loft? No. We were lucky.

The London costumiers, Morris Angel & Sons, had exactly the right

clothes for us. We hired them for one night so that we could try out the new Cockney medley at a special cabaret that we were going to do at the Dorchester Hotel. It went well, so we arranged with Angels to lengthen the term of hire to one week. Experimenting with the medley, each time we did it, the audience appreciation became better and better. We continued to hire for a further one month. By then, we knew that our new cockney routine was a winner. Or was it? In case it was a fluke, we arranged to hire the costumes for six months so that we could have the use of them till the end of our summer season. That was the autumn of 1961. Now, in 1988, we still have those costumes. We have paid more in hire charges over the years than if we had had them made to measure. Whatever we have paid, we have had a marvellous bargain. Those Pearlie King and Queen costumes have been our friends, our workmates and an investment. They've shared applause with us all over the world. From the London Palladium to the Glasgow Alhambra in Britain, the O'Keefe Centre in Toronto, Canada, to the Pacific Ocean on the QE2.

One day soon, when we retire, we shall have to return those dear old cockney costumes to the firm that owns them.

They've given a lot of pleasure to us and audiences all over the world. Eventually they will leave our wardrobe.

They'll never leave our hearts.

ADELE LEIGH

In January 1975 my husband presented his credentials to the Queen as Austrian Ambassador to the Court of St James. I accompanied him to the Palace, albeit in the Embassy car, while he drove from Belgrave Square in the official horse-drawn carriage.

My dress was made for me especially for the occasion by my Viennese dressmaker, Poldi. After combing every possible fashion magazine, we finally decided on a burnt-orange coloured wool with a polo neck and very full bishop sleeves. I had a matching hat made by a milliner of great repute in London, Reed Crawford – a wonderful concoction of chiffon and feathers.

I felt like a million dollars as we walked into the throne room, and I made a really deep, operetta-type curtsey – bent head – the lot!

However, when I raised my head, I saw to my great surprise that Her Majesty was wearing a dress in burnt-orange wool with bishop sleeves, too! I think I detected a rather quizzical look on the royal face as we moved forward for our audience!

LYNDA BARON

A dress! Just after the war, in Manchester, there was no such thing. Even if you had had the wherewithal to buy one, it would have been called a frock, and boy, did I want a frock. The sort that would convince an old-fashioned Mum that I could wear stockings and suspenders with it, to make it look just the thing. (Whilst I'm on the subject, who was the spoil-sport who invented tights? Most men would have him or her hung!!) But I digress. We went off to C & A Modes to buy me a nylon organza frock. It was full-skirted, with horizontal stripes of brown, maroon and gold, with a gold trim. I thought I looked the bee's knees. In fact, at 5 feet 7 inches, weighing 7 ½ stone, with legs like an under-nourished pony and with cotton-wool in my bra to help out my non-existent bosom (if you can believe that), I must have looked like a deckchair on stilts.

Thus attired, and with my gold dancing shoes in a brown paper bag, I set off for the Locarno Ballroom. Well ... I wasn't to know that my date had a motor-bike. So there's me riding pillion! In an effort to stop my precious frock from creasing too much, I put my feet on the ground at the traffic-lights. When they changed to green, my date and the bike roared off, leaving me standing in the middle of the road. What really hurt was that he didn't notice for about five hundred yards, by which time I was stomping off in high dudgeon!!

GILLIAN BEVAN

I was in my third job. Joan Knight at Perth Theatre had decided I had 'range' and therefore had me in every show in the season for ten months without a break. At the time I thought it was a compliment, but I realize now it was just economics – I was on Equity minimum. However, I learnt more from Joan about the general business of stagecraft than from anyone else since.

There was a low spot, however, during the winter (the worst Scotland had seen for fifty years). The Crieff road was blocked by snow, so for three weeks I'd been sleeping on people's floors, unable to get to my digs. The pipes were frozen, so we were all pretty smelly. I was rehearsing *Look Back in Anger* in the mornings with Patrick Sandford, *Armstrong's Last Goodnight* in the afternoons with Andrew McKinnon, and about to open in my first panto, *Robinson Crusoe*, as the Fairy – 'Fairy Coraline, the Fairy of the Deep', in more ways than one. . . .

My costume was a cross between a sort of nautical Boadicea and King Canute. I had a very large and unwieldy trident, and a mammoth train that was basically a large fishing net with assorted shells and bits of seaweed stuck on it. I had never worked so hard in my life, and to top it all I'd got the ubiquitous winter 'flu. (The stage management would jokingly put out a call after beginners saying that 'Miss Bevan appears by kind permission of Lemsip and Beecham's Powders.) With all the catarrh in my head I'd gone completely deaf, unable to hear anything from a distance of further than ten feet, but my aches and pains eased somewhat during the excitement of the technical rehearsal as the joys of pantomime wizardry were laid open to me. I'd never seen dry ice before - there were buckets of it strategically placed around the wings for my 'underwater ballet' – and the DSM [Deputy Stage Manager] had casually mentioned that in order to make it look as though I had appeared as if by magic I had to rush on to my mark as soon as the flash box had gone off. Not wishing to show my ignorance I nodded sagely, not having a clue what a flash box was, but thinking I'd busk my way through it.

In this instance the flash box had been a bit recalcitrant so unbeknown to anyone the determined electrician had put twice the charge of explosive in to give a really good flash effect.

I was in the wings trying to strip by brain of John Osborne and 16th-century Scots, when the thing went off. I rushed on to my mark, stood directly above the box, and set about reciting my rhyming couplets with gusto. I was dimly aware of Joan in the distance waving at the stage as though conducting traffic, but desperate to appear a 'pro' I carried on, vaguely conscious that the smoke effect was winding its way round me. Ah, the magic of theatre, I thought, they must be using the dry ice in this scene as well.

They weren't. It was smoke. A flame from the flash box had ignited my fishing net frock and was subsequently melting the plastic crabs attatched thereto. In my catarrhal haze I was completely deaf to the cries of warning, but the dry ice buckets of water came into their own and the stage manager drenched me with one and effectively put me out. I'm proud to have been the one and only pyrotechnic fairy in the history of Perth panto!

JULIA McKENZIE

Clothing-coupons didn't really run to tap-dancing outfits ...so the photo here is an ingenious blend of net curtains and safely-stored sequins, all fashioned by my mother. I was quite proud of this, as you can gather by the 'aren't I the bee's knees?' look in the eyes, although frankly I wouldn't have remembered it except for this picture. But one coat I had, that was made for Sunday Best, by a 'real dressmaker', will be emblazoned on my memory forever.

It was thick, woolly and white, with an 'adorable' pink Peter Pan collar and cuffs and covered buttons, and one of those poke-bonnets only a mother could love. I immediately didn't like the feel of it when it was put on me, but I was paraded in front of my grandmother. 'Isn't it pretty?' I heard my mother say, 'You'd never know it was made from a Witney blanket, would you?'

I remember my arms stiffening with embarrassment. Then I threw myself on the floor with childish rage. (Costume designers who have worked with me may recognize this little failing.) Anyway, I don't think I was put in it again. It was probably given away to some other unfortunate child to sport on Sundays.

The moral of this tale is: don't put your daughter in a Witney blanket, Mrs Worthington. She might throw herself on the floor, get a taste for the dramatic, and end up on the stage.

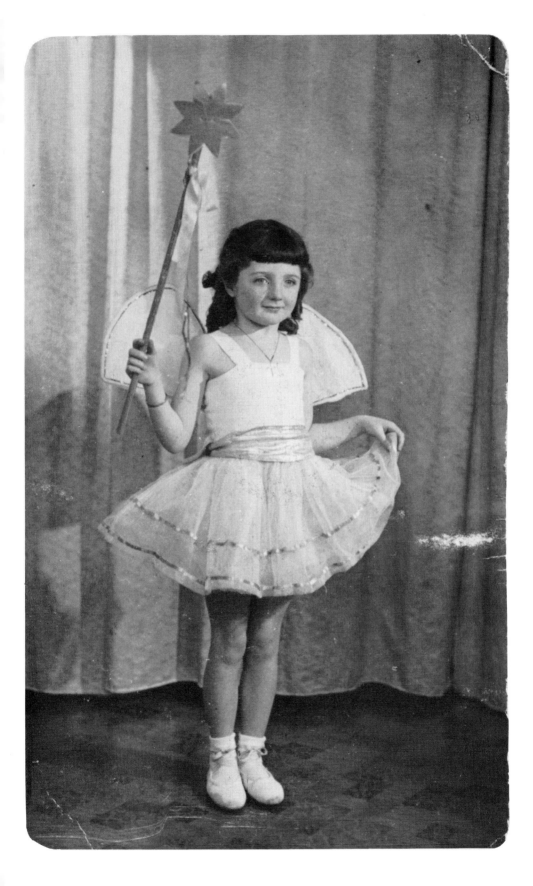

HOPE JACKMAN

I won't mention the year, but it was a long time ago – my first audition for a touring musical. They were short of one girl. I was fourteen years old, and looked it. My hair was straight and short, ('cut it to show the tips of her ears,' my mother used to say). I wanted to look grown up, like the chorus girls I had seen, so I wore my mother's coat and dress, with a toque hat to match, in a beautiful fine turquoise angora wool material. The long-sleeved dress was, of course, too long, as was the three-quarter length coat, with a small grey squared Peter Pan collar, but that did not deter me at all.

I will always remember my first audition outfit with a smile. I think, on looking back, the producer must have had a warm heart – because, I got the job!

JOSEPHINE GORDON

On my fifth birthday my Father gave me a very pretty pink silk organza party dress. Pink ribbons were threaded through, and the fine material was delicately decorated with a small fern design.

After each party the dress was packed away in tissue paper in a big box.

It was still in beautiful condition, though now too small for me, when my Father asked for its return. I was devastated and many a tear was shed before I finally had to give it up. He told me of this poor deprived little girl that he knew of in the East End. It was her birthday, and he thought her need was greater now than mine.

I never got over it, and to this day I remember with a pang that beautiful party dress.

160